HEARTS
of GOLD

Stories of Courage,
Dedication and
Triumph from
Canadian Olympians

LORNE ZEILER

RAINCOAST BOOKS
Vancouver

To Ari and Brian, the boys I grew up with;
And to Shari and Avery,
the girls who prove that I still have a lot of growing up to do.

Raincoast Books gratefully acknowledges the ongoing support of the Canada Council for the Arts; the British Columbia Arts Council; and the and the Government of Canada through Department of Canadian Heritage Book Publishing Industry Development Program (BPIDP).

Cover and interior design by Teresa Bubela
Photo credits on page 160
Front cover: (clockwise, from left) Gaétan Boucher and Ethel Catherwood © CSHF; Jaime Salé and David Pelletier © Fred Lum/*The Globe and Mail*; Sylvie Fréchette © Bernard Brault
Back cover: (from left) Percy Williams and Alwyn Morris © CSHF; Sharon Donnelly by Mike Ridewood; Silken Laumann © CSHF

NATIONAL LIBRARY OF CANADA CATALOGUING IN PUBLICATION DATA

Zeiler, Lorne
    Hearts of gold : stories of courage, dedication and triumph from Canadian Olympic athletes / Lorne Zeiler.

Includes index.
ISBN 1-55192-684-9

    1. Athletes — Canada — Biography. 2. Courage. 3. Olympics — History — 20th century. I. Title.

GV697.A1Z44 2004   796'.092'271   C2003-906950-8

LIBRARY OF CONGRESS CATALOGUE NUMBER: 2004090399

Raincoast Books   *In the United States:*
9050 Shaughnessy Street   Publishers Group West
Vancouver, British Columbia   1700 Fourth Street
Canada   V6P 6E5   Berkeley, California
www.raincoast.com   94710

Printed in Canada by Friesens

10 9 8 7 6 5 4 3 2 1

CONTENTS

PREFACE

THE IDEA FOR THIS BOOK came to me from two different sources: watching a Canadian boxer fight with a broken right hand and watching my brother battle a serious illness.

Egerton Marcus displayed one of the most heroic acts I have ever seen from an athlete. Even though his dominant hand was broken and extremely swollen, he fought aggressively and returned home with a silver medal. I started thinking that there must be many Canadian athletes who had demonstrated similar sacrifice, courage, determination or sportsmanship in their sporting lives.

In the winter of 2002, I thought back to my idea for this book. I was also reminded of my older brother, Ari, and my ambition to write a book that captured his spirit. Ari was my best friend and hero growing up. Unfortunately, he developed ulcerative colitis as a teenager. He underwent surgery, but never healed properly. The day before his 21st birthday, Ari was diagnosed with a brain tumor. Soon after, Ari was hit with meningitis ventriculitis — spinal fluid build-up — and his brain tumor proved cancerous. His determined battle to fight off these many diseases made me realize how truly precious life is. Ari Mark Zeiler passed away a few months later.

Courage brings its own unique rewards. For many of the athletes profiled in this book, unyielding determination resulted in an Olympic medal. For others, it meant giving a top performance under trying circumstances, and for one athlete, it even meant forfeiting his right to compete so that he could stand up for what he believed was right. My brother's struggle was inspiring and gave my family and his friends an opportunity to say thank you and goodbye.

Sport has the ability to bring out the best in all of us. I can not think of better role models for my own daughter and other Canadians than the athletes in this book. I hope that their stories will inspire a new generation of competitors and encourage the spectator to learn more about the athletes representing our country in Athens and beyond.

— Lorne Zeiler, January 2004

FOREWORD

ONCE THE LAST finish line is crossed, the sweat wiped away and the roar of the crowd is gone, what truly remains is the heart of the Olympian. It is a heart that when filled with passion, tenacity and a commitment to excellence, can help an athlete overcome the greatest of obstacles.

Through this inspiring book, we journey into the heart, mind and soul of twenty Canadian Olympians. They dared to dream and push the limits of human possibility for the common goal of Olympic glory. Their challenges and triumphs provide us with messages of hope, perseverance and personal understanding that can be used in all areas of our lives.

Sport can be a powerful force for personal motivation and social change. The universal principles of the Olympics help to promote fair-play, culture and peace. These ideals are rehearsed everyday on the playing field, and my fellow Olympians you meet in this book exemplify them wholeheartedly.

I believe that courage and strength of character also lie in the hearts of those who see beyond themselves and contribute to making our world a better place by their example. Such was the courage and character of my late parents. As my role models, they lived as silent heroes to the fullest, even through their own pain and illness later in life. Surrounded by the love of family and friends, they showed me how strong the power of one can be.

The lessons I have learned from my own longstanding career as an Olympian have been applied throughout my life after sport. The foundations of a solid work ethic and an unrelenting will are what drive athletes to success. However, this is never more important than when giving something back. As Olympians, we are often called upon to give our hearts to our community, and it is a role that many, such as myself, proudly embrace.

Those with hearts of gold can be found everywhere in our communities. Let us celebrate them as national icons who give us a glimpse of what it means to be truly golden.

— Charmaine Crooks, Olympian

Chapter One

HONOURABLE
CONDUCT

LAWRENCE (LARRY) LEMIEUX

Lifesaver

"I saw the head of the second crew member bobbing in the water.
He was far away from the boat … I decided that I better do something."

LARRY LEMIEUX

THE RACING CONDITIONS in South Korea on day five of the Finn-class Olympic sailing final were treacherous. Canadian yachtsman Larry Lemieux was in the midst of navigating his boat to the finish line when he noticed a capsized boat from a previous race in the water. One of its crew members was holding onto the vessel, but the other was stranded out of the sight of rescue crews and contending with the rough, breaking waves. Lemieux quickly made up his mind. He pulled out of the race to bring the stranded sailor back to his boat, found the craft's rudder to turn the boat over and helped the pair get to shore. Though Lemieux ended up in 11th place overall, he made his mark in Olympic competition by saving Joseph Chan's life.

Larry Lemieux, born on November 12, 1955, in Edmonton, Alberta, took up sailing shortly after he learned to run. As the youngest of eight, Larry always wanted to be like his older brothers, who frequently sailed the waters of Lake Wabamun near their cottage. At age five, he took a sailboat out on his own for the first time. A gust of wind capsized his boat and because he was not heavy enough to turn the boat over on his own Larry had to be rescued by his brothers. By the time he was nine, his mother realized that Larry was not going to stay away from the water,

Sailor Larry Lemieux arrives on shore after completing the fifth race of the Finn-class yachting competition at the 1988 Olympic Games in Seoul.

so she enrolled him in sailing school. Though the minimum age was typically 11, Larry was accepted based on his experience and ability. Within two years, Lemieux was racing nationally. By the time he was 16, Larry had fully caught the sailing bug; he travelled the country to competitions with his sailboat strapped to the roof of his mother's car.

The 1976 Olympics in Montreal were a turning point in Lemieux's career. Fifty new Finn-class sailboats had been purchased for the Olympic Games. After the competition, each of the single-operated, 4.4 metre, 120-kilogram boats was given away to local Canadian sailors. Lemieux was one of the lucky recipients. Within two years, Larry made the national team, skippering his own Finn. He also managed to place within the top five in the world in both 1978 and 1980. Lemieux also trained and raced in two-person boats. In 1984, when he finished poorly in the Olympic qualifying competition in the Finn class, he partnered with Wito Guessing in the larger two-person boat in the Star class and won a spot on the Canadian Olympic team. At the Games the team placed 10th overall. During this time, Lemieux spent the winters working odd jobs — from serving, to construction, to assembly line labour — so he could train and race in the summers.

In 1988, Lemieux was the top-ranked Finn-class sailor in Canada and represented the country at the Olympic Games in Seoul, South Korea. Olympic sailing races and regulations are designed to ensure that the winner of the race is determined by his or her skill level, not boat design. The boats for each sailing class must be the same precise weight and size and be made from the same materials and have the same method of construction. Each competition comprises numerous races held on the same course over a period of days and requires the skipper to use all points of sail. In 1988, the Olympic regatta consisted of seven days of competitions, one each day that lasted between two and two-and-a-half hours. The individual or team's top six race results were then added together to determine the final standings, with the lowest score winning. To return home with a medal, competitors needed to achieve consistent top results.

During the first day of competition in Seoul, Lemieux aggressively manoeuvred his boat and finished in first place. On day two, he earned a respectable fifth place, but then had problems in the third and fourth races, finishing 22nd and 13th respectively. On the fifth day of races the

*The courageous Larry Lemieux is presented with a symbolic award by IOC President
Juan Antonio Samaranch for his heroic rescue of Korean sailor Joseph Chan.*

weather conditions were horrible. There was a powerful wind and a strong
current in the water between Korea and Japan. Steep waves were breaking
offshore in the middle of the race course. Lemieux, an experienced skipper,
boldly pushed forward. He quickly took the lead, but was passed about
halfway through the race by two boats. He moved back into second place
just past the halfway point and was headed toward a top three finish.

Visibility was poor, but Lemieux pushed on. Surveying the water,
Lemieux noticed a capsized two-person boat, a 470 class that had drifted
well off course. He spotted one member of the crew hanging on to the
boat, but his partner had been pushed far away by the strong current and
crashing waves. Rescue crews were unlikely to spot the sailboat and were
even less likely to notice the stranded sailor, Joseph Chan, because they
were contending with their own problems. Their boats were too fragile
to push through the rough water and most of the drivers had little experience with such treacherous conditions.

Lemieux decided that he had to pull out of the race to help these
sailors. First he picked up the stranded sailor and began manoeuvring his

Finn to the capsized 470 and the other sailor. Lemieux then found the 470's rudder so they'd be able to turn the boat over. Lemieux's boat was too small to support two other sailors, particularly in the treacherous weather conditions, so he waited with them until further help could arrive. It was Larry's own coach, Pat Healy, who came to the rescue. Healy had been concerned that Lemieux seemed to have disappeared from the race, so he had taken out a heavier boat to search for Larry. The Canadian coach towed the two sailors to shore. Lemieux returned to the course and finished 21st for the day.

After the race, Larry launched a protest regarding his placing and the two sailors stayed by him as the Olympic Association ruled on his appeal. Lemieux was awarded a second place finish for race five because he was racing in second place before he pulled out to save the stranded sailors. Before the competition the next day, the media bombarded Larry with questions and interviews. Larry was unable to concentrate on racing and finished 13th and 21st in his final two races. He placed 11th overall during his second Olympic competition.

Larry Lemieux did not receive a medal at the Olympic Games, but he was given a symbolic award for placing the life of a fellow sailor above race results. In a private ceremony, Juan Antonio Samaranch, the president of the International Olympic Committee, presented Larry with a porcelain jar bearing the Olympic insignia.

Lemieux continued to compete successfully after the Seoul Olympics. He won the gold medal at the 1991 Pan-American Games in Havana, Cuba. Though he did not qualify for the Canadian Olympic team in 1992, he managed a second place finish in the World Cup held that year in Greece, and he unofficially retired in 1993. Lemieux's success in subsequent competitions, which he took part in solely for fun, earned him the right to join the national team. He declined the honour on each occasion. Larry now spends more time designing Finn-class boats than racing them. As a boat designer and a freelance coach, Larry travels to international competitions, including the Olympic Games. He lives with his girlfriend in Milton, Ontario.

Larry Lemieux went to Seoul, South Korea, with the ambition of becoming an Olympic hero by winning a medal. Instead he became a hero for a completely selfless reason: he saved the life of a fellow competitor.

Larry Lemieux skippers his Finn-class sailboat into the sunset.

"HIS STYLE OF RUNNING, IT WAS CERTAINLY EFFECTIVE IN GETTING HIM ALMOST TO THE GOLD. NOT QUITE, BUT ALMOST TO THE GOLD."

CANADIAN OLYMPIC HURDLER JIM WORRALL

PHIL
EDWARDS

Good as Gold

DR. PHIL EDWARDS is likely the most precious sports import Canada has ever received. From his first summer Olympic Games in 1928 until his last in 1936, Edwards, the gentleman and steadfast competitor, took home five Olympic bronze medals and eight top six showings — more medals than any Canadian Summer Olympics athlete ever. Edwards was drawn to Canada not by a desire for a better life, however, but by his desire to compete. He wanted to train with the best in track-and-field and to compete internationally — particularly at the Olympic Games.

Born on August 28, 1907, Phil Edwards was the 12th of 13 children born to Fitzgerald Edwards, a wealthy magistrate in British Guyana. Phil developed a love for running and competition at a young age. His father recognized Phil's ability and determination, and decided to take on the roles of coach and running partner. Under his father's training, Edwards became a champion middle-distance runner in his teens. At that time, however, British Guyana had little to offer runners in terms of training or competition, so in 1926 Phil decided to move to the United States. He attended New York University and trained under the famous track coach Von Elling. With a fluid, natural style, Edwards soon began setting inter-collegiate records. Though his times were fast enough for him to compete

From 1928 to 1936, Phil Edwards won five bronze medals. He was Canada's most decorated Olympic athlete.

at the 1928 Olympics, Edwards faced a bigger hurdle in getting there — his nationality. He couldn't compete as an American since he was a British subject, and his native British Guyana didn't have an Olympic team.

His solution came in the form of an invitation from Bobby Robinson, the Canadian founder of the British Empire Games (later called the Commonwealth Games). Robinson had seen Edwards run and knew of his talent; he invited him to join the 1928 Canadian Olympic team, and Edwards gladly accepted. At the Games in Amsterdam, Phil competed in three track events: the 400-metre, the 800-metre and as a member of the four-by-400-metre relay team. In the relay, Edwards, with the help of his teammates, James Ball, Alexander Wilson and Stanley Glover, won his first of many bronze medals.

When Edwards graduated from New York University, he decided to study medicine. But he wanted a school that offered a top-rate medical program as well as an excellent track program. McGill University was a natural choice. Phil Edwards' confidence, calmness, and love of sports and competition soon won over his teammates; he became the captain of the McGill track team from 1931 to 1936. As his friend and fellow teammate Jim Worrall explained, "Phil was the backbone of the McGill team. Phil was an outstanding human being … He was a team player" (*The Olympians*, CBC-TV). Phil was supportive of his teammates and would often push them to run in the lead with him and then would fall back at the last few metres to let his teammate win.

Phil Edwards was one of 130 athletes whom Canada sent to the 1932 Games in Los Angeles. This time Edwards was also entered in three races: the 800-metre, 1,500-metre and four-by-400-metre relay. His running strategy was to break from the pack early in the race, build on his lead and then try to hold off any late sprints from his competitors at the finish. Edwards was successful in setting the pace early in both the 800-metre and 1,500-metre competitions. But in both races, he tired and ultimately failed to hold off all the competitors down the stretch. He won two bronze medals. In the 800-metre, Phil led most of the way, but was overtaken by two runners in the final turn. In the 1,500-metre, he set a torrid pace, again leading through most of the course, but was caught and passed by two runners in the final 100 metres. Edwards had to use all

Phil Edwards (second from left) competes in an athletics event at the 1932 Los Angeles Olympics. Edwards won bronze medals in the 800- and 1,500-metre.

of his remaining strength to hold off the American favourite, Glenn Cunningham, to win his third bronze medal. Edwards also won another bronze medal as a member of four-by-400-metre relay team.

Phil Edwards was the only athlete entered in both the 800-metre and 1,500 metre track events. Many sports historians feel that Edwards may have won the gold in the 1,500 metre race had the 800-metre run previously not taken so much energy from him.

Phil Edwards competed in numerous track events outside the Olympics, as a member of both the Canadian team and the British Guyanese team. One of his shining moments in track was as a member of the British Guyanese team in 1934. Edwards won the 880-yard race and became the first black man to receive a gold medal at the British Empire Games. When the 1936 Games were held in Hitler's Nazi Germany, Edwards decided to put politics aside to focus on competition. He competed in three events again, and was also selected as the captain of the Canadian track team.

Edwards started the 800-metre competition in his typical way, racing out to the lead and then setting a fast pace for his challengers. But just as

Throughout his career, Edwards competed for both British Guyana, his birthplace, and Canada, his adopted homeland.

in 1932, Edwards could not hold on to the lead. John Woodruff, the American favourite, challenged Edwards for most of the race, overtaking him in the middle. Edwards did regain the lead, but was again passed by Woodruff in the last half lap, and then by yet another runner. It was a familiar story for Edwards, another third place finish.

Edwards' next competition was the 1,500-metre race in a field over-flowing with talented runners. While he did finish fifth, he never challenged for a medal and is likely better remembered for gallantly stepping aside in the middle of the race when New Zealand runner Jack Lovelock passed him and claimed Olympic gold. The four-by-400 track team also came up just short of a medal, finishing fourth, only a nose behind the German team. Phil Edwards' count of Olympic medals, all bronze, would end at five.

For his great contribution to Canadian sports, Edwards was awarded the first-ever Lou Marsh Award as Canada's outstanding athlete in 1936. But a greater victory may have come when his Canadian teammates made a stand on his behalf at a hotel in London, England. During their return trip from Berlin, the exhausted team stopped in London to spend the night. The athletes were unpacking their bags when they heard that the hotel staff had refused to rent a room to Edwards, because of the colour of his skin. The team decided to leave en masse to show its support for Edwards. Cathleen Hughes-Hallett, a fencer, echoed the sentiment of the whole team when she said, "If this hotel is too good for Phil Edwards, it's too good for me" (*The Olympians*, CBC-TV).

After the Olympics, Phil Edwards graduated from McGill as a specialist in tropical diseases and joined the staff of the Royal Victoria Hospital in Montreal. Edwards also chose to serve for his adopted homeland. During World War II, he was a captain with the Canadian armed forces. After the war, he participated in and led numerous international missions, particularly to countries in dire need of medical attention. Dr. Edwards also became one of the world authorities in his field, tropical diseases. He died on September 6, 1971, at the age of 64 from heart problems.

To commemorate his great contribution to Canadian track-and-field, the Phil Edwards Memorial Trophy was established shortly after his death. The trophy is presented annually to Canada's most outstanding track athlete. Phil Edwards was also elected to Canada's Sports Hall of Fame in 1997, but only after a vigorous campaign from fellow inductee Jim Worrall. While Edwards never won a medal higher than bronze at the Olympics, he proved over his lifetime that he had a heart of gold. His legacy of five medals and eight top six finishes over three Olympic Games remain a testament to his natural athletic abilities and love of competition.

ALWYN
MORRIS

Too Small to Compete?

"We had made a mistake and we were not going to make it again."

ALWYN MORRIS BEFORE THE 1,000-METRE K2
(TWO-PERSON KAYAKING) FINAL

WHEN ALWYN MORRIS was first told by the aboriginal reserve's canoeing coaches that he was too small to compete, he quit the team. Morris returned to practices three weeks later, but only on the insistence of his friends and because of a commitment that he made to his grand father. Over the next three years, Morris worked hard. He made the reserve's team, switched to kayaking and became a member of the Canadian national team in 1975. But he would have to wait nine years for an opportunity to compete at the Olympics. In 1984, Alwyn Morris and partner Hugh Fisher were selected to compete at the Los Angeles Games and they were determined to return home with a medal. Instead, they collected two, a bronze in the 500-metre K2 and Canada's first-ever gold medal in kayaking for the 1,000-metre K2 race. Morris has used his positive experiences to be an ambassador for sports in the Native community and a role model for Canada's aboriginal youth.

Alwyn Morris was born on November 22, 1957, at the Kahnawake Reserve in the province of Quebec. As a child, he was a big sports fan and was influenced by his grandfather, who had been a standout athlete during his adolescence. On the reserve where Alwyn lived, the only organized sports were hockey and lacrosse. Morris enjoyed lacrosse, but

Alwyn Morris (right) and Hugh Fisher celebrate a gold medal win in the men's K2 kayak event at the 1984 Olympic Games in Los Angeles. Alwyn raises an eagle's feather as a symbol of his Mohawk heritage and as a tribute to his grandfather.

when he was 12 years old, the program was cancelled. The reserve elders were convinced that sports could have a positive effect on the youth in their community, so they searched for affordable alternatives. Their territory was situated near water and the Grand Trunk boat club had recently disbanded and was willing to part with its war canoes at bargain prices, so the reserve chose canoeing.

In the program's first year, the 13-year-old Morris was excited to get involved. The coaches were less enthusiastic. They told Alwyn that he was too short and not strong enough to be a competitive canoeist. Morris was disappointed and stopped attending practices. But he didn't stay away for long — Morris had learned from his grandfather that success in athletics required dedication, perseverance and sacrifice. After some persuasion from his friends, Alwyn returned to the team and quickly proved the coaches wrong by making the reserve's team the next season.

Morris' introduction to competitive canoeing was not promising. He fell out of the canoe during his first race and was disqualified. Fortunately for Morris, the reserve invested in another sport that suited him better — kayaking. His progress was rapid — during his first full year of competition, his K4 (four-person kayak) team qualified for the Canadian Championships and finished in the top 10. By 1975, Alwyn Morris earned himself a place on the Canadian national team. But when he was not selected to represent Canada in the 1976 Olympic Games in Montreal, Morris decided that to be competitive he needed to step up his training. He moved to British Columbia, where he could train year round with the top Canadian athletes in the sport.

Morris focused on solo competitions (K1) and the K4. Because of his strength and stamina, and his training, Alwyn had the unique ability to succeed at both short-distance sprint races, such as the 500- and 1,000-metre, and long-distance endurance races, like the 10,000-metre. By 1980, Morris had proven his ability as a soloist and team kayaker by winning numerous national championships and placing prominently in international competitions. However, like all other Canadian athletes, he would not compete at the Olympics in Moscow because the Canadian government decided to boycott the Games due to the Cold War.

A young Alwyn Morris shares a laugh with his grandfather, one of his first role models.

In 1982, Morris was asked to take the place of injured paddler Dennis Barré in Canada's top K2 (two-person kayaking) team. At six feet two inches, Morris' new partner, Hugh Fisher, towered over the muscular five-foot-nine inch Morris, but the two athletes complemented each other in the boat and they gelled quickly. Within a couple of months, Morris and Fisher won an international meet in Hungary, took a top three placing in Germany and finished second in the World Championships. They continued to perform well in 1983, finishing in the top six in most races. Morris also made history as the only North American ever to win the long-distance 10,000-metre race at the Moscow International Regatta. The next year, Alwyn Morris would get his long-awaited Olympic opportunity when he was selected, along with Hugh Fisher, to represent Canada at the Los Angeles Games.

The pair's first race was the K2 500-metre. They easily qualified for the final and were favourites to win a medal. But during the race, they didn't get off to as strong a start as they had hoped. They lost valuable seconds

Alwyn Morris (left) and Hugh Fisher's strong, synchronized strokes power the confident pair to the finish line in a kayaking event at the 1984 Olympic Games in Los Angeles.

from the start to the transition phase and they were in fifth place at the halfway point. They managed to recover and move up to second place during the last 100 metres. But in the final few strokes the Canadians were overtaken by the Swedish team, which pulled ahead to capture the silver medal. Morris and Fisher had to be satisfied with bronze.

The Canadian pair had little time to recover before the 1,000-metre final the next day. They spent most of the afternoon discussing the race and devising their strategy for the next day's competition. Morris and Fisher concluded that, based on the field of competitors, if they could be at the halfway point of the race by 1:40 to 1:41, they could win the race. They executed exactly to plan. At the halfway point, the team was in fourth place with a time of 1:40.02, but during the second half of the race, the other pairs faded. Morris and Fisher maintained their stroke rate and took the lead — they won the gold with a time of 3:24.22 — 1.75 seconds faster than the nearest team. During the medal presentation ceremony, Morris held up an eagle's feather that he had received from a group of aboriginals living in California to share his victory with his grandfather and the Mohawk people.

After the Olympics, Morris continued to compete, but he also became actively involved in the aboriginal community. He travelled across the country promoting the benefits of sports and education for aboriginal communities. During these trips, Morris realized that there was only a small number of aboriginal athletes competing at the top amateur levels because of a lack of sports infrastructure within the communities themselves. He began working with a number of other leaders in Canada's aboriginal community to build the foundations of the Aboriginal Sports Circle (ASC), which was formally established in 1995. In addition to being one of the main organizers, Morris was one of the key lobbyists for the cause. The ASC's aim is to use sports as a means of "preventing many of the social ills facing Aboriginal peoples, and foster community healing" by creating "more accessible and equitable sport and recreation opportunities for Aboriginal peoples" (www.aboriginalsportcircle.ca). He also became actively involved with the North American Indigenous Games, which offers aboriginal youth across North America the opportunity to compete and learn more about their culture. The Games have grown from 3,000 athletes and numerous cultural performers in 1990 to 6,000 athletes and 3,000 cultural performers at the 2002 Games in Winnipeg, Manitoba.

In 1987, Hugh Fisher came out of unofficial retirement and asked Morris to compete with him again, hoping that they could qualify for the 1988 Olympic Games. Morris eagerly accepted and moved back to British Columbia to train, even though he was still recovering from Epstein-Barr syndrome, a virus that is similar to but that can be much more severe than mononucleosis. They trained hard, without a coach, and qualified for the Olympic Games being held in Seoul, South Korea, despite Morris also suffering a stomach ulcer. They would not repeat their 1984 performance, however; the pair were eliminated in the one event they entered, the 500-metre K2.

Both Alwyn Morris and Hugh Fisher were inducted into the Canadian Sports Hall of Fame and both were presented with the Order of Canada.

Alwyn Morris continues to be actively involved in both sports and his community as chairman of the Aboriginal Sports Circle — a position he's held since its inception in 1995. Morris lives with his wife and two children at Kahnawakee Reserve.

Alwyn Morris proved that heart and determination can overcome size and muscle mass. His achievement of one gold and one bronze medal remains the best Canadian performance in Olympic kayaking. Morris hopes that his achievements and the work of the ASC will lead other aboriginal athletes to aspire to similar successes and to develop a love for sports in the process.

Chapter Two

STAYING
ON TRACK

CHRISSY
REDDEN

Racing Flat Out

"When I looked down to my front wheel, it confirmed one of my worst fears — I had a slow leak."

CHRISSY REDDEN

MOUNTAIN BIKER Chrissy Redden arrived in Sydney, Australia, for the 2000 Summer Olympic Games with three goals: to be fully prepared for all race conditions, to compete to the best of her abilities and to capture a medal. While she did achieve her first two objectives, a technical glitch during the race cost her the third — a chance at an Olympic medal. During the second lap of the five-circuit final, Redden was climbing a hill when her tire went flat. It cost her precious time to fix it, but Chrissy stayed calm and focused. Her discipline enabled her to quickly repair the tire, remount her bike and attack the rest of the course. She passed numerous riders along the way and finished in the top 10.

Chrissy Redden was born on March 16, 1966, in Campbellville, Ontario. A competitive athlete, she had had some success in cross-country running in high school and cross-country skiing in university, but did not discover her passion until she got on a mountain bike for the first time. While in university, Redden often saw her friends return from mountain bike rides covered in mud, but exhilarated by the experience. Chrissy bought an entry level bike and started to join them on rides. She was hooked from the start — she revelled in the thrill of riding over logs,

Chrissy Redden battles uphill during the women's mountain biking final at the 2000 Olympic Games in Sydney.

rocks, roots, attacking difficult hills and charging down technical descents. She even started participating in local races.

Redden continued to seek out more information about the sport and what competitions were available, including the national team trials. By 1994, Redden achieved her first goal: she joined the national team and competed in her first World Championship in Vail, Colorado. As her results continued to improve, Redden's competitive drive grew stronger.

In 1996, mountain biking became an official Olympic event. In the first-ever women's Olympic race in Atlanta, Canada's Alison Sydor earned a silver medal. Unfortunately, Redden, who had only been riding for five years and was still pursuing another career, did not make the Olympic team. The next season, she decided that the only way she could compete with the best women mountain bike riders in the world was if she trained full-time. She quit her job as a quality assurance manager and set her sights on the 2000 Olympic Games in Sydney, Australia. In 1997, her full-time training schedule included up to 20 hours a week of aerobic exercises, weights, yoga and course work. But the hard work paid off; Redden yielded consistent top results in all of the international competitions she entered that year.

Mountain biking requires a high level of stamina and superior technical skill to navigate the intricate and physically demanding courses. Through hard work and consistent training, Redden built up both her physical strength and her endurance. She also improved her technical skills, ably navigating the climbs and descents of the most difficult courses. By 1999, she was ranked in the top ten in overall Union Cycliste Internationale (UCI — the international sports body governing cycling) world ranking. That same year, Redden became the Canadian national champion for both cross-country mountain bike racing and another similar sport, cyclo-cross racing. Cyclo-cross combines mountain biking with intervals of running with your bicycle, to overcome large obstacles that cannot be traversed on a bicycle. Redden was also named by *Canadian Cyclist* magazine as the female Cyclist of the Year. She had also recently placed second in a World Cup competition in Mount St. Anne, Quebec. When she arrived in Sydney, Australia, for the 2000 Olympic Games, Redden was expected to challenge for a medal.

On September 23, 2000, the top 29 women riders in the world lined up to start the Olympic women's mountain biking competition. The race consisted of five loops of a very challenging 8.1-kilometre course. Many competitors exploded from the start, leaving Redden in a pursuit role from the first lap. This was not ideal for her since passing in a mountain bike race can be extremely challenging. A rider's starting position is often crucial to her race results. The course is designed for a single biker, so the track is quite narrow. Competitors must use momentum, technical skills and timing to move ahead of riders who try to block them from passing. During the second lap, Redden began to make her move. But as she began to climb, she noticed that her front wheel was not pushing forward as fast as she expected. When she looked down, her fear was confirmed: her front tire had a slow leak.

Though she would lose precious time, Redden immediately dismounted and set to work on her tire, which needed to be fixed if she were to finish the race. Instead of succumbing to frustration and despair, Redden stayed focused. She had prepared for such an unfortunate incident, since competitors cannot receive any outside assistance during a race; they must perform all bike repairs on their own. Redden worked quickly. She tried to block out thoughts that she had just lost any chance of winning an Olympic medal and focused on fixing the tire as fast as possible so she could get back into the race.

By the time she got back on her bike, a number of riders had passed her. Redden finished her second lap in 15th place, well behind the leaders. She concentrated on using the skills that she had developed to give her best performance and pass as many riders as possible along the way. She attacked the course aggressively, powering up hills, speeding through descents and waiting for the right moment to pass all riders within her view. She made up for lost time and crossed the finish line in eighth place. Her final time of 1:54:7.38 was only about four-and-a-half minutes behind the winner, Paola Pezzo of Italy.

Shortly after the Olympics, Redden went into the record books, but not for biking. She is in the *Guinness Book of World Records* for the quickest ascent of the tallest free-standing building in the world. In a publicity stunt for Toronto's unsuccessful 2008 Olympic bid, a number of Canadian athletes climbed the CN Tower. Redden finished first.

Chrissy Redden races to the finish after fixing a flat tire that cost her precious time during the mountain biking competition at the Sydney Olympic Games.

Chrissy Redden continues to train for the 2004 Olympic Games in Athens, where she hopes to win Canada's second medal in women's mountain biking. Since Sydney, she has captured numerous World Cup medals and the 2002 gold medal at the Commonwealth Games in Manchester, England. Her husband, Chris, and the Canadian team's national coach, Yuri Kashrin, remain two of her strongest supporters.

The misfortune of suffering a flat tire during Olympic competition could have crushed a lesser athlete. Instead, Chrissy Redden showed strength and demonstrated the skills that led to her Olympic team selection. Her calmness under pressure; her ability to focus on repairing her bike, not on her dream of an Olympic medal slipping away; and her tenacity and aggressive riding led to a heroic, top 10 finish.

The day after the competition, Redden's race was further put into perspective as her tire went flat again; this time it could not be easily fixed. Redden's repair had held long enough for her to complete the course and finish the race a champion.

SHARON
DONNELLY

Completing the Course

"I knew I was going down! All I could think of was getting back into the race."

SHARON DONNELLY

AFTER YEARS OF training and sacrifice, Sharon Donnelly had made it to the 2000 Olympic Games in Sydney, Australia, to compete in the first-ever Olympic women's triathlon. But disaster struck during the bike phase of the competition. When two women crashed directly in front of her, Donnelly was forced to brake hard and was thrown from her bike. She managed to keep her focus while she came to terms with the reality that she no longer had a chance to challenge for a medal. She picked herself up, changed her bike's punctured tire and continued on. In both physical and emotional pain, Donnelly managed to finish the race. Even though she came in 38th place, Sharon Donnelly crossed that finish line a true champion.

Born on July 29, 1967, in Toronto, Ontario, Sharon Donnelly developed a passion for sports at a young age. Donnelly's parents enrolled her in gymnastics and her brother in swimming. But Sharon, wanting to be like her brother, asked to take part in swimming as well. By the time she was 13 she made the national team and the next year she was the top Canadian swimmer for her age group in the 100-metre butterfly. But when she did not qualify for the Canadian Olympic team in 1984, Donnelly decided to quit. She could not see herself devoting the next four years of her life to training for the next Olympics. She also could

Sharon Donnelly celebrates her gold medal win at the 1999 Pan Am Games in Winnipeg.

Sharon maintains her focus coming out of the transition area in the Murakami ITU International Triathalon in Japan. She finished seventh in the race.

not justify the economic sacrifices that her family would have to bear since money was already tight.

Donnelly enrolled in the Canadian Royal Military College a couple of years later, because the school offered free tuition, a guaranteed job and a significant amount of sports and athletics. During a basic training session, Donnelly discovered a new talent. Though she had never run competitively before then, she completed a long-distance run well ahead of all the other female freshman students and was recruited for the cross-country team. Although she did not enjoy the training, Donnelly loved the competition.

During the summer after her third year of college, a friend asked Donnelly to race in a triathlon — a race which combines swimming, bicycling and running. Even though she did not own a bicycle, the race interested her. A typical triathalon consists of a 1.5-kilometre swim, a 40-kilometre ride and a 10-kilometre run. Sharon fell in love with the sport during her first competition and completed two more races that summer. During the next year, the RMC decided to send a contingent to the World

. Military Athletic Championships. Donnelly and a colleague represented the college and finished first and second respectively in the women's triathlon, largely because they were the only entrants. Traditionally, the event was for male participants only, but since the Canadian women had travelled all the way to Belgium, they were allowed to compete as well.

After graduation, Sharon was posted at the Borden base in Ontario, where she befriended a mountain biking partner and the man she'd later marry, Dave. The next year, she was posted to Ottawa, where she was able to take advantage of running and swim clubs and well-marked bike trails for consistent training. During that two-year posting, she managed to finish in the top five in nearly all of the triathlons she entered.

The events of 1995 would be the turning point in Donnelly's career. Sharon had already considered leaving the army because the government was downsizing the military and was offering generous buy-out packages. Then she found out that her next posting would be to Bosnia as part of a peacekeeping force. At the same time, she learned that the International Olympic Committee had decided to make the triathlon an official Olympic event in 2000. Sharon decided to retire from the army and move to Ottawa to train for the Olympics in Sydney.

Donnelly concluded that to make her name known on the international circuit, she needed to compete internationally, so she entered a competition in Japan. She finished seventh. After the race, the president of the International Triathlon Federation approached her and offered to subsidize her training. The money was well spent — Donnelly's results continued to improve once she was able to devote her full attention to the sport. During the 1998/1999 and 1999/2000 seasons, Donnelly spent the winters training in Australia. The result of this decision included a second place finish in a major race in Monte Carlo and a victory at the 1999 Pan-American Games. When she arrived in Sydney for the 2000 Olympic Games, Sharon was ranked 10th in the world and was considered to have a legitimate chance at a medal.

But events turned against her even before the race began. Sharon was given a starting placement on the far side of the diving pontoon, far away from most of the top-ranked women. Though the swimming segment was typically her strongest leg of the race, Donnelly struggled with the

A courageous Sharon Donnelly smiles at Canadian fans as she crosses the finish line at the Games in Sydney.

poor starting position and fought through choppy waters to finish behind the first pack of racers. Donnelly's pack tried to establish a quick pace in the cycling portion to challenge the leading group of riders. After the first of six laps, her pack was gaining valuable time on the leaders. The cycling stage consisted of six circuits of a 6.6-kilometre course. During the second lap, two cyclists directly in front of Sharon touched wheels and crashed. Sharon had no time to react — she was travelling over 40 kilometres per hour — so she squeezed her brakes and prayed that the fall would not be too hard. She toppled from the bike into the barrier and then to the pavement, smashing her back wheel in the process. In that instant, Donnelly's Olympic dream seemed to evaporate.

When the bruised and bloodied athlete got to her feet, she realized that she had broken her bike's rear tire. She needed to get the wheel fixed as quickly as possible so that she didn't get lapped by the leaders or she would be disqualified. She began running with her bike until a race official offered to change her tire. Donnelly tried to calm her nerves and focus on not getting passed by the leaders. When she finally mounted her bike, she put all the pain aside to push on and stay ahead of the leaders' group that was not far behind. When she began the final 10-kilometre run in last place, only encouragement from fans and her own stubborn determination kept her going to the finish line. Tears of pain and frustration streamed from her eyes for the entire distance.

Of the 11 women who crashed, only two actually completed the course. Sharon finished in 38th place, ahead of the other fallen athlete. While she physically healed from the fall, phone calls and e-mails from proud and concerned Canadians helped her recover emotionally from the hard luck that can occur in this kind of competition.

Donnelly continues to train for the 2004 Olympics in Athens with fellow Canadian Jill Savege, the winner of the 2003 Pan-American gold medal, and with numerous members of the British women's team. Her husband, Dave, a career military officer, and her mother, who had carted Sharon around to swimming practices, remain her biggest supporters.

Sharon Donnelly was able to complete her first women's Olympic triathlon competition because her mental toughness was equal to her physical ability. The crash and subsequent fall cost Donnelly the chance to win an Olympic medal. But she earned her own personal victory by rising up against pain and despair to finish the race.

Chapter Three

OVERCOMING
PHYSICAL
ADVERSITY

SILKEN
LAUMANN

Remarkable Recovery

"I told the doctor who insisted that I wouldn't be able to compete
in Barcelona that I thought differently."

SILKEN LAUMANN

JUST WEEKS BEFORE the 1992 Olympics, Silken Laumann suffered a
leg injury so severe that doctors wondered if she would ever walk again.
The 1991 and 1992 world champion in 2,000-metre single sculls rowing
was unlikely to be out of her wheelchair before the Olympic Games in
Barcelona. But Laumann proved that a determined mind can help heal
muscles, tendons and ligaments. Miraculously, she made it to the Games
and engineered a come-from-behind sprint to capture the bronze medal
and the hearts of the Canadian people.

Silken Laumann was born on November 14, 1964, in Mississauga,
Ontario. She inherited a love for both the outdoors and sports from
her father, to whom she was very close. But she came to rowing almost
by accident. During her grade 11 year, Silken, a middle-distance runner,
suffered an injury and needed to take up another activity to maintain
her fitness during her recovery. To please her older sister, a member of
the Canadian national rowing team, Silken took up rowing and picked
up the sport quite quickly. She'd had a tremendous growth spurt during
high school that had proven awkward for running, but her now five-
foot 11-inch frame and athletic build were the perfect combination

*Silken Laumann proudly displays her medal after her courageous performance
in the single-sculls competition at the 1992 Summer Olympic Games in Barcelona.*

for rowing. Her height gave her additional leverage and reach to produce powerful strokes that could win races. She paired with her sister, Danielle, and within a year Laumann became a member of the Canadian national team. And only a year later, the sisters captured a bronze medal at the 1984 Los Angeles Summer Games in the double sculls event. Silken Laumann was already an Olympic medalist and not even 20 years old.

Laumann pursued her career as a rower and remained one of the top competitors in North America during the mid to late 1980s, but she rarely placed in the medals on the world stage. She was a determined competitor, which often led to fights with her new double sculls partner, Kaye Worthington. The two placed seventh in the 1988 Summer Olympics in Seoul, missing the opportunity to compete in the final. Disheartened, Laumann actually contemplated retiring from the sport in 1989 when she took a full-time job as a publicist for Penguin Books. She soon realized, however, that she missed the challenge and focus that came with rowing competitively.

In 1990, the Canadian men's rowing team staged a coup by landing one of top rowing coaches in the world, Mike Spracklen. Silken Laumann, then the top-ranked female single sculls rower in Canada, decided that if she wanted gold, she needed to train with the best. Within weeks, she had packed her bags and moved across the country from Mississauga to Victoria, British Columbia. Her decision paid instant dividends; only five months later, Laumann came second at the 1990 World Championships, a tremendous improvement from her seventh place finish in 1989. She went on to capture first place in both the 1991 and 1992 World Championships in the 2,000-metre single sculls event. She was poised for Olympic gold at Barcelona. Then the unthinkable happened.

On May 16, 1992, during a regatta in Essen, Germany, a men's doubles team, which was warming up for its race, sliced right through Silken's shell and then through the calf of her right leg. With her boat 2.5 kilometres from shore, Laumann's first concern was for her life. But after the rescue crew picked her up and took her to shore, Laumann's next worry was whether she was going to lose her leg — tendons, muscles and nerves were dangling from her lower leg and she could see her broken bone.

Silken Laumann raises her arms in victory after being awarded the gold medal in single-sculls rowing at the 1991 World Championships in Vienna, Austria.

In fact, her injury looked so gruesome that one of the rowers who had hit her passed out when he saw it.

While she was being rushed to the trauma centre, Laumann told teammate and companion John Wallace that she did not want to miss the Olympics. It must have seemed an impossible dream with the Barcelona Games only two months away and only 78 days before the women's single sculls final. Silken returned to British Columbia, where she had five reconstructive operations in 10 days and had a sixth scheduled for after the Olympics. Medical experts anticipated she'd need a minimum eight months of rehabilitation, but the Olympics were now only weeks away.

A determined Silken Laumann began to train. Because she was in excellent physical condition at the time of the accident, her muscles and tendons healed faster than expected. Because the boat would support the weight of her body, placing less strain on her joints, she was also able to row even before she could walk. Silken had members of the men's team lift her from her wheelchair and then lower her into her shell so she could row. Her technique quickly returned, as did her speed and confidence. With extraordinary ambition, drive and stubborn determination, Silken proved doctors wrong and prepared herself for Barcelona.

Even though she walked through the Olympic village with a cane and a heavily bandaged right leg, Laumann successfully completed her qualifying heat on July 28 and even won her semi-final heat on August 1st. This placed her in the 2,000-metre single sculls final to take place the next morning. From the start, Laumann looked strong, but as the competitors reached the 1,000-metre halfway point, it became obvious that Laumann's amazing recovery would not result in gold. Romania's Elisabeta Lipa and Belgium's Annelies Baedael pulled away from other rowers to take first and second place. Laumann and American Ann Marden would have to fight it out for the bronze. Marden made her move with 500 metres remaining and pulled ahead of Laumann — an Olympic medal of any colour now seemed out of reach. But Laumann, who had already increased her strokes-per-minute rate to an incredible 38 for the last 500 metres, dug deep, summoned all of her energy and increased her stroke rate once again to 40 strokes per minute for the last 200 metres.

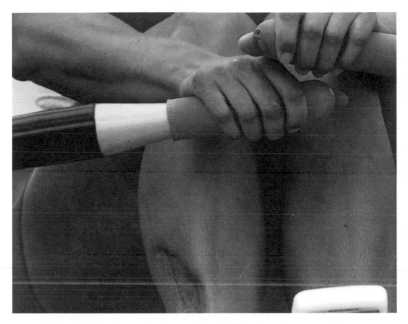

Four years after the accident that nearly ended her career, the scar on Silken Laumann's right calf remains a symbol of her courage and spirit.

She rowed past Marden and captured the bronze medal. Laumann's inner strength, focus and excellent conditioning secured her place on that podium.

Silken Laumann returned to Canada as a national hero. She had been given the honour of Canadian flag bearer for the closing ceremonies and received a gold medal and plaque from the people of Canada in honour of her extraordinary performance. Soon after the Olympics, Laumann underwent her sixth and then seventh operations on her right leg. She became an inspirational speaker and spokesperson, and she continued to row. Even though a double false start disqualified her during the 1994 World Championships, Silken still captured gold in the single sculls events in the Netherlands, Great Britain, Belgium and Switzerland during 1994 and 1995. She took the singles gold at the 1995 Pan-American Games in Argentina, and was then thrust into the spotlight only a few days later for a positive drug test. Laumann had been taking Benadryl, the medication suggested by team doctors to relieve her cold. Unfortunately she was unaware that it contained the banned substance pseudoephedrine, a synthetic match to the stimulant ephedrine. Even though it was the only positive test she'd had in her career and the traces found of the drug were minimal, the women's fours team was stripped of its gold medal. Silken showed her grace and maturity by weathering the media storm. She continued to focus on the 1996 Atlanta Summer Games, her last chance at Olympic gold. At 31, Laumann was still in excellent physical condition and was one of the top rowers in the world, but she had passed the age when most rowers reach their peak.

Laumann again qualified for the Olympic final in 1996. For most of the race it looked as if she would capture Olympic gold, as she led her closest rival, Yekaterina Khodotovich of Belarus, at the 1,000-metre and 1,500-metre marks. Unfortunately, Khodotovich had more strength left at the end and made a strong kick during the final 500 metres to pull ahead of Laumann and capture the gold. Laumann graciously accepted her silver medal. This was her last competitive race and she officially retired on March 16, 1999.

Because of the inner strength and spirit that she displayed in 1992, Silken Laumann is a sought-after motivational speaker and widely followed freelance writer. She has received honorary PhDs from the Universities of Victoria, Windsor and McMaster. The three-time Olympic medalist was a former Lou Marsh Award winner as Canada's outstanding amateur athlete; twice awarded Canadian Female Athlete of the Year; inducted to the Canadian Sports Hall of Fame in 1998; received the Thomas Keller Medal in 1999 for an outstanding career in rowing; and was named Canadian of the Year by the Canadian Club in 1992. In Mississauga a street has been named in her honour, and in Victoria a flower, the Silken Laumann rose, bears her name. Despite all the accolades and accomplishments, Laumann now finds raising her two children to be her most important work.

In 1992, Laumann's determination defied reason and her recovery captured a nation's imagination. Her story continues to inspire future athletes to achieve.

Silken Laumann is now one of Canada's most inspirational leaders, a highly recognized and beloved Canadian athlete.

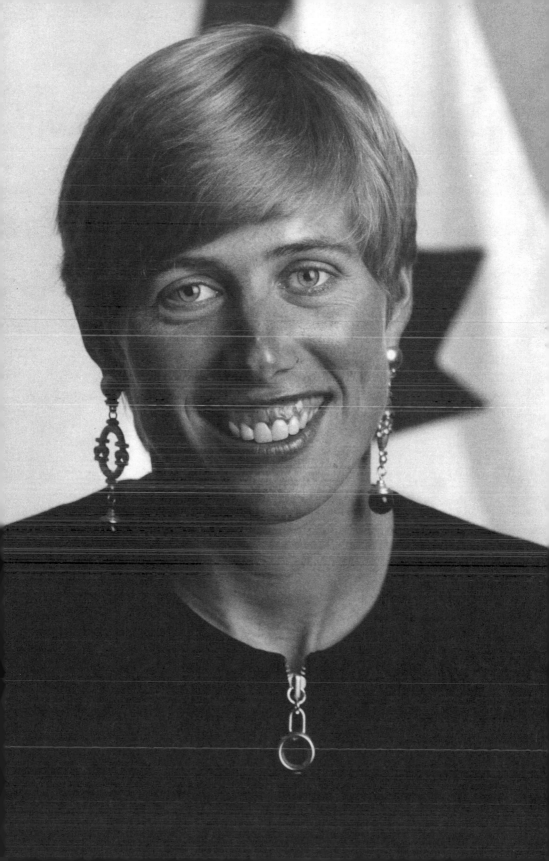

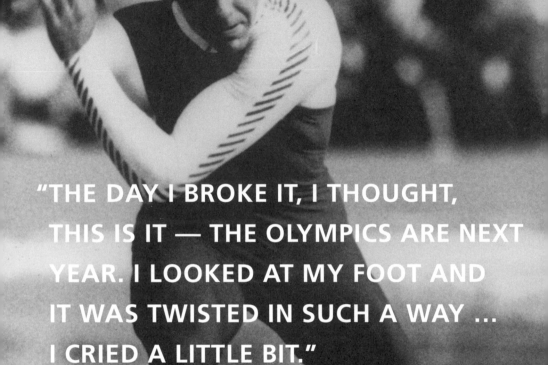

"THE DAY I BROKE IT, I THOUGHT,
THIS IS IT — THE OLYMPICS ARE NEXT
YEAR. I LOOKED AT MY FOOT AND
IT WAS TWISTED IN SUCH A WAY ...
I CRIED A LITTLE BIT."

GAÉTAN BOUCHER ON BREAKING HIS ANKLE TEN MONTHS
BEFORE THE OLYMPIC GAMES IN 1984

GAÉTAN BOUCHER

Speed Skating's Spokesperson

"If I can do it [win gold], it will attract a lot of attention and that should give the sport a boost."

GAÉTAN BOUCHER AT SARAJEVO OLYMPIC GAMES, 1984

AS A TEENAGER, Gaétan Boucher decided to put away his hockey stick and focus on another sport, one that was little-known in most of Canada: speed skating. By 1983, his dedicated training and tenacity had already won the small skater from Quebec a silver medal at the 1980 Winter Olympic Games and numerous World Championship medals. But with no Olympic gold to his name, Boucher felt unfulfilled. He was also disappointed that speed skating was still a marginal sport in Canada outside Quebec. Then, only 10 months before the 1984 Winter Olympics in Sarajevo, Yugoslavia, Boucher shattered his ankle in a short-track speed-skating training session. When his ankle finally healed, it had less strength and reduced flexibility. This did not stop Boucher from realizing his dream. Of the four Olympic medals Canada earned at the 1984 Winter Games, Gaétan Boucher won three, including two gold. And the sport of speed skating also won national attention and hard-earned support.

Born in the Quebec City suburb of Charlesbourgh, on May 10, 1958, Gaétan Boucher learned how to skate in a backyard rink that his father, Cyrenus, had constructed. He did not take to the sport immediately. In fact, though he was put on the ice at age five, Boucher did not skate again until after he turned nine, when he began playing hockey. He quickly

Gaétan Boucher's fierce determination at the 1984 Winter Games in Sarajevo won him three medals: two gold and one bronze.

realized, however, that his late start made him a weaker skater than most of the other kids. When he saw an advertisement at his school for a speed-skating club, Gaétan thought it would be a good opportunity to improve his skating skills and make him a better hockey player. Although he finished poorly in his first few races, Boucher was soon returning home from competitions with trophy after trophy. By 1973, Boucher, only in his mid-teens, became a member of the national speed-skating team. He soon gave up hockey to focus solely on speed skating.

In 1976, Gaétan Boucher was selected as a member of the Canadian Olympic team that would compete in Innsbruck, Austria. He placed in the top 15 in all three of the races he entered, including a sixth place finish in his best event, the 1,000-metre. Gaétan continued to focus on his training and was again selected for the 1980 Olympic team in Lake Placid, U.S.A. But it soon became apparent that the best any speed skater from outside the U.S. could hope for was a silver medal. Leading up to Lake Placid, American skater Eric Heiden was dominating the sport. Heiden's long, powerful legs and six-foot-one, 185-pound frame propelled him along the track to win gold in all distances short and long: 500-metre, 1,000-metre, 1,500-metre, 5,000-metre and 10,000-metre.

Long-track speed skating pits two skaters against each other as they race against the clock. One skater starts in the inside lane of the circular 400-metre track and the other in the outside lane. Both skaters must cross over the lanes once each lap, so they actually skate half of the lap in the inside lane and half in the outside lane. Boucher knew that a faster partner often leads to faster times for both skaters. If he could draw Heiden as his pairs competitor for the two-and-a-half lap, 1,000-metre race, he had a chance at a medal. At five foot nine and 150 pounds, the much smaller Boucher lost to Heiden by 1.5 seconds, but his time was more than two-tenths of a second faster than all other competitors'. He returned home with a silver medal, the highest medal awarded to a Canadian at the 1980 Games.

During the next season, Eric Heiden retired and Gaétan Boucher began to establish himself as the man to beat by setting two world records in Davos, Switzerland. He also won the samalog sprint, a competition which adds a skater's two fastest 500-metre and 1,000-metre times

Gaétan Boucher and Canadian bobsledding legend Vic Emery in the press box at the 1984 Winter Olympic Games in Sarajevo.

to produce a combined score. Boucher was the first skater ever to attain a score below 150, a feat even skating great Eric Heiden never achieved.

Even though he was one of the smallest skaters on the international circuit, Boucher consistently achieved top rankings because of his quest for perfection in every skating movement. He was determined to attain the most speed and distance from each stride. But Gaétan Boucher had another hurdle to overcome in his efforts to succeed in speed skating. Because it was a marginal sport in Canada, Boucher didn't even have the luxury of being able to practise on a speed-skating oval in his home country. As a result, he frequently travelled to Lake Placid, New York, and Inzell, West Germany, to train.

Boucher also had success in short-track speed skating. He was the only athlete to skate on both the long-track and short-track Canadian teams. Short-track speed skating is a race against other skaters, not a clock. A pack of skaters, usually six, compete on a 111-metre circular track, so control on turns is essential for success. Skaters must win a series of heats to earn a place in the final pack. Boucher won the World

*Gaétan Boucher celebrates after winning his first medal of the 1984 Winter Olympic Games —
a bronze in the 500-metre speed-skating event.*

Short-Track Championships twice and came in second three times. In 1992,
short-track skating became an official Olympic event.

Boucher continued to show his prowess on the ice by winning the
500-metre World Championship and placing second in the samalog
sprint in 1982. Unfortunately, however, 1983 would not be as good a
year. Boucher finished out of the medals at the World Championships.
Then, only 10 months before the 1984 Olympic Games, Gaétan Boucher
had an accident that would jeopardize his chance of winning an
Olympic medal. During a short-track training session, Boucher was
turning a corner at maximum speed when his boot rubbed the ice —
he fell on top of his foot and crashed into the boards. His foot twisted
180 degrees, fracturing his ankle in three places and tearing the ligaments
surrounding his ankle.

The damage was so severe that doctors first wondered if Boucher
would be able to walk again. They were, however, able to surgically
repair his ankle to some degree. Though Boucher would not have the
same flexibility as before, his ankle would be well enough for him to

compete in the Olympics. He would also need to take six weeks off from practice to let the ankle heal. Over the previous seven years, Boucher's longest period of inactivity had been only a total of three weeks. Through pain, frustration and hard work, Boucher returned to form and was selected as the Canadian team flag bearer for the 1984 Sarajevo Winter Olympic Games.

Boucher's first race was his weakest event, the 500-metre. But he managed to win a bronze medal in a very tight field. His next race was his specialty, the 1,000-metre. He was so confident of his abilities that he told the media there was no way he could lose. He was also hopeful that a gold medal victory would attract new fans and athletes to the sport in Canada. His closest competitor, Russian Sergei Khlebnikov, stood over six feet tall and weighed over 200 pounds. But Boucher's powerful strides and determination more than compensated for Khlebnikov's height and weight advantage. Boucher posted a time of 1:15.80, more than eight-tenths of a second faster than Khlebnikov, taking his first Olympic gold medal.

The next day was the three and 3.75-lap 1,500-metre competition and Boucher felt that he had a solid chance of winning another gold medal. Boucher again had the luxury of skating in one of the last heats. Before he hit the ice, he saw that the fastest time was just under one minute 59 seconds, posted by Khlebnikov, the favourite. He knew that he still had a chance. Boucher got into his starting crouch, but nerves and a trembling knee cost him a false start. On his second attempt, Gaétan got away cleanly and his smooth, powerful strides carried him to the fastest lap times of the day. But by the end of the first lap, he could already feel his legs getting stiff. The fatigue and burning pain in his legs worsened with each lap. By the time he started his fourth and final lap, he was "pushing only on guts and determination" (*Toronto Sun*, February 17). Boucher took another gold through sheer tenacity and heart, and in doing so made long-track speed skating Canada's sport.

After the Sarajevo Olympics, Boucher kept skating. His success continued in 1985 with a second place finish in the sprint samalog and a gold medal in the 500-metre at the World Championships. But his ankle injury flared up again. Scar tissue had built up around his ankle and the ligaments had never healed properly, leaving them stiff and weak. Even though he had some of the scar tissue surgically removed, his left ankle was not able to fully support his powerful skating strides. Boucher would likely have retired, except that the 1988 Winter Olympics were going to be held on Canadian soil in Calgary, Alberta. Boucher was selected for the team and competed in his fourth Olympic Games. He proved that he was still competitive with the best, but was no longer in the top tier. He finished 14th in the 500-metre, fifth in the 1,000-metre and, in the final competitive race of his career, he finished 14th in the 1,500-metre. The Canadian crowd gave him a standing ovation for his effort and for what he had done for both his country and his sport.

Gaétan Boucher attained the kind of sporting success that few other Canadians can even dream of achieving. For his four Olympic medals and countless World Championship medals in both long- and short-track speed skating, Boucher was awarded the Lou Marsh trophy as the top amateur athlete in Canada in 1981 and 1984. He was also named the Quebec athlete of the 1980s. He became a Member and then an Officer of the Order of Canada in 1983 and 1984. Saint-Hubert, the town where he grew up, has since named a school, street and arena in his honour. Boucher continues to earn his living in sports, but uses his marketing degree from Hautes Études Commerciales as much as his background in skating for his work in product development for BauerNike's in-line skate division. He is also the vice-president of Quebec's University Sports Foundation. Outside athletics, Boucher is husband to Karin and father of four: three boys and a girl.

Many of his competitors from outside Canada likely wish that Gaétan Boucher had never decided to put away his shin pads and hockey stick to focus on speed skating. Boucher's heart and hard work allowed him to overcome the obstacles of his smaller stature and a broken ankle to win Olympic gold. Boucher's extraordinary victories have had a much greater impact than temporary feelings of national pride in Canada. Since the late 1980s, Canadians, yearning to replicate the glory of Gaétan Boucher, have won dozens of World Championship and Olympic medals and have established Canada as a powerhouse in both long-track and short-track speed skating.

Gaétan Boucher received many awards to mark his distinguished athletic career and his contributions to the community, province and country.

ELVIS
STOJKO

Medal of Bravery

"Pain is short-lived, but pride lasts a lifetime."

ELVIS STOJKO, 1998

ELVIS STOJKO WAS DENIED an Olympic medal in 1992, won silver in 1994 and arrived in Nagano, Japan, for the 1998 Winter Olympics as the reigning world champion and one of the favourites for the gold medal. Though few people knew, Elvis was also fighting the flu and had suffered an agonizing groin injury less than a month before the Olympic Games. Miraculously, however, Elvis was able to block out his physical suffering to skate an energetic short program and a clean long program. Unfortunately it was not enough to win the gold medal. Stojko took home a silver medal and the satisfaction that he had given everything to the competition.

When Irene Stojko gave birth to her third child on March 22, 1972, in Richmond Hill, Ontario, she knew that he was going to be special, so she named him Elvis. As his biggest fan and supporter, she would devote much of her life to helping to ensure that her prophecy came true. Elvis Stojko found his vocation early on in life. When he was three years old, Elvis watched a figure skating performance. He was so awed and inspired by all the spinning he saw that he decided he wanted to be a figure skater. Within a couple of years, Elvis Stojko stepped onto the ice for the first time wearing figure skates that his mother had painted black.

Elvis Stojko competes in the figure skating event at the 1998 Nagano Winter Olympics.

Elvis took to the sport right away and showed great promise. While he was still in primary school, Elvis was sent to Ellen Burka, a leading coach at that time, to develop his skills and artistry. Working with Ellen, Elvis improved significantly, but it didn't all go smoothly. Elvis had strong opinions on both the music that he wanted to use in his performance and on how his routines should be choreographed. Their disagreements led Elvis to his next coach, Doug Leigh. The pair would work together for more than 15 years.

While Elvis was developing his figure skating skills, his father worried that he might get teased at school for his choice of sport. He decided that Elvis should take up karate so that he could defend himself. This began Elvis' affection for the martial arts and East Asian culture. The sport taught him discipline and helped with his figure skating performance by further developing his strength, form and focus. Elvis received his black belt at age 16. He then began training in kung fu because the circular motions used in many of the techniques could be translated well into figure skating. Many of Stojko's performances have included martial-arts-inspired music, themes, dress and movements.

Elvis Stojko won the 1988 Canadian Junior National Championships when he was 16. He moved on to the senior amateur level and began his long battle with Kurt Browning for the title of Canadian champion. Elvis came second from 1990 to 1993 and then captured the title in 1994. With the exception of 1995, when he withdrew because of injury, Stojko continued to win the Canadian title every year until his first retirement in 2002.

On the international stage, Elvis displayed his superior technical skills and moved up the ranks quickly. At the 1992 Winter Olympic Games in Albertville, France, he skated the only clean short and long programs, even with a stress fracture in his left foot. Unfortunately, Elvis finished in seventh place. Some argue that his scores were lower because the international judges were reluctant to accept his more masculine interpretation of figure skating and because he had a lower international ranking coming into the Games.

Stojko continued to challenge at the World Championships, performing programs with greater and greater degrees of difficulty. He became celebrated as the first skater to land a "quad," a jump that includes four rotations prior to landing, in combination. Stojko was awarded the silver medal at the 1994 Olympic Games in Norway, and won the Worlds in 1994, 1995 and 1997.

As the reigning world champion, Elvis Stojko arrived in Nagano for the 1998 Winter Olympic Games as the favourite to win a gold medal. Unfortunately, he also arrived with new obstacles to overcome. He thought he was suffering from jet lag, but it turned into the flu and a high fever. He was also suffering from an injury that had still not healed. At the Canadian Championships one month earlier, Elvis had twisted a nerve in his groin and torn an abductor muscle in his lower abdomen. He worked hard to conceal his weaknesses so as not to give his competitors an advantage. He purposely chose to live outside the Olympic village and skipped some practices to stay in bed. He cut other practices short and attempted fewer jumps to conserve his energy to fight his illness and not cause any further strain on his groin or lower abdomen.

In the short program, a skater performs eight required movements within his or her two-minute-and-40-second program. The choreographed routine is set to music and includes sequences of steps or footwork, spins, jumps and jump combinations. When Elvis Stojko took to the ice to perform his routine, he skated with such flair and accuracy, attaining great height in his jumps and remaining flawless in his landings, that it was impossible to tell that he was in anything but top form.

Heading into the final, Elvis was in second place trailing his main rival, Ilia Kulik, from Russia. But Elvis' illness and full-out performance had taken a toll on his body. He had reaggravated his groin and abdomen injury — the muscles were extremely overworked and the area around his nerve had became further inflamed and tender. The pain was exacerbated every time Elvis attempted a jump because he would push off from his foot, extend his legs, use his stomach muscles to pull them through the rotations and then drive them back quickly for a clean landing. In the three days before the final, Elvis was given acupuncture treatments each day to alleviate the pain and reduce the swelling.

The long program is the skaters' chance to shine. With no required movements, routines are choreographed to best display each skater's own

Elvis Stojko grimaces in pain following his routine during the men's free skate competition at the Winter Olympics in Nagano, Japan.

technique and artistic skills. For the four-minute-and-30-second long program, Stojko was scheduled to skate last in his grouping of five skaters. Once Elvis saw Ilia Kulik's long program, he must have known that his own chances for a gold medal were slim. The Russian landed a quadruple toe loop and eight triple jumps, each cleanly and with near perfect presentation. When Elvis took to the ice, he was forced to reduce the level of difficulty in his program due to his condition. When he attempted his first quad, he could feel that there was not enough power in his legs for four revolutions, so he reduced his jumps to three (triple) or two (double) revolutions; he also removed some of the more difficult movements to reduce pressure on his lower abdomen. Somehow, despite agonizing pain, he had enough concentration, experience and strength to land each of his jumps cleanly. When he finished, Elvis' face told the story — for the first time he could admit to the world the pain that he had endured over the past few days. Grimacing, Elvis was helped off the ice by his coach, Doug Leigh, and choreographer Uschi Keszler. When the medals were presented shortly after, Elvis Stojko walked to the podium to receive his silver medal wearing running shoes — a first in Olympic figure skating history.

Elvis skipped the World Championships that year to repair the nerve in his groin area and to let his abdominal muscle heal, but returned to competition the next season. Though he continued to dominate at the national level, his results at world events began to slip. At the 2002 Olympic Winter Games in Salt Lake City, he finished in eighth place. Elvis felt that he didn't have the same intensity or drive for competition — soon after Salt Lake, he decided to turn professional. He became a commentator for CTV and continued to perform by touring in his own show, "Elvis on Ice," and in "Champions on Ice." In April 2003, Elvis Stojko announced his return to active competition, marking a fifth chance at an Olympic gold medal. Unfortunately, six months later, on September 26th, 2004, Elvis announced his retirement from amateur competition. Stojko is now concentrating on a career as a professional skater.

Elvis Stojko was awarded the Norton H. Crowe Award for Athlete of the Year by the Canadian Sports Council in 1994 and 1997 and the Lionel Conacher Award for Athlete of the Year by the Canadian Press in 1994.

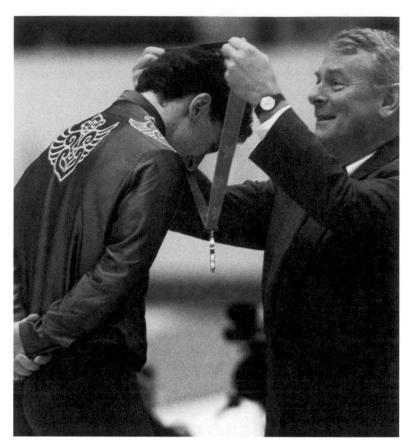

Elvis Stojko receives the silver medal from Canadian IOC member Dick Pound at the figure skating event at the 1998 Nagano Winter Olympic Games.

He is known as the first skater to achieve many technical milestones in competitive skating, such as landing a quadruple jump combination as well as a quad/triple. Because he was able to stay in top competitive form for many years, Elvis ties with Dick Button of the United States for the most World Championship medals won since World War II — six. Elvis has acted as the Kids Ambassador for Ronald McDonald Children's Charities since 1994 and was chosen the Gillette world champion in 1998, an award given to an athlete for achievement in sport and humanitarian contributions to the community. Stojko was also the sole recipient of the Governor General's Meritorious Service Cross in 1998 for his outstanding service to Canada, and he was inducted into the Skate Canada Hall of Fame in 2004.

Elvis Stojko's aim has been to push himself to achieve perfection in his performances and to make a difference in both his sport and himself as an individual. He has taken the technical component of figure skating to a higher level by innovating quadruple toe combination jumps and by choreographing and completing some of the most physically demanding routines ever skated. Elvis' performance at Nagano was the ultimate sacrifice of his body, but it allowed him to achieve victory on his own terms.

ANNE
OTTENBRITE

Accident Prone

"All I could do was lie there and look at the ceiling and think 'No
Olympics,' all that work for nothing."

ANNE OTTENBRITE ON DISLOCATING HER KNEE ON MAY 21, 1984

WHEN ANNE OTTENBRITE kicked up her leg to show a friend the
deck shoes that she was wearing, she never imagined such a usually
harmless move could have such grave consequences. She heard a pop in
her knee and suffered an injury that threatened her chances of competing
in the 1984 Olympic Games. Although Anne's dislocated knee forced her
to skip the Olympic trials, Trevor Tiffany, the Canadian swim team's head
coach, made the unprecedented decision that Ottenbrite, Canada's top
female swimmer, would still join the team and compete at the Olympic
Games. His decision was proven right — Ottenbrite won three medals in
Los Angeles: a bronze, silver and Canada's first-ever Olympic gold medal
in women's swimming.

Anne Ottenbrite was born on May 12, 1966, in Whitby, Ontario. She
was introduced to swimming when she was only three years old and her
father tossed her into the backyard pool. Anne soon developed a powerful whip-kick while trying to swim away from her father, Joseph, who
would chase her in the pool pretending to be a shark. When Anne was
10, the Olympic Games were held in Montreal. She was captivated
watching the Games on her black and white television. Though she did
not participate in any competitive sports at the time, she made a

*Anne Ottenbrite proudly listens to the playing of her national anthem after winning a gold
medal in the 200-metre breaststroke at the 1984 Summer Olympic Games in Los Angeles.*

promise to herself that she was going to go to the Olympic Games and win gold. After trying out numerous sports, Anne joined a summer swimming league in 1978. She demonstrated real promise in breaststroke and was recruited by coach Lynn Trimbee to swim with the Oshawa Athletic Club the following year.

Anne continued to flourish under Trimbee. In 1981, she began training with the Ajax Swim Club and a new coach, Paul Meronen, who continued to develop her unique and powerful whip-kick style. In breaststroke, the swimmer propels herself forward by moving both her arms and legs through the water in circular motions. While the arms pull, the legs push the swimmer along in a circular whip-like fashion. In the whip-kick the swimmer brings her feet together bent at the knees with her heels almost touching her bottom. Then she thrusts both legs out and around in a circular, pushing motion until her two feet come together again fully extended. Because Ottenbrite was also double jointed, she was able to thrust her torso in the air at the beginning of her whip-kick. This action helped her gain more distance with each kick, but also brought her toes out of the water.

At age 14, Ottenbrite was invited to compete at the Canada Games where she set the Canadian junior record for the 200-metre breaststroke. She also won a spot on the Canadian national swim team. She earned a reputation both for her grace and athletic ability in the pool, and for her lack of those qualities out of the water. Accidents seemed to happen to Anne everywhere she went. During training camp in Hawaii, Anne tripped coming out of a convenience store and cut open her left elbow. At the 1982 Commonwealth Games, Anne was so involved giggling with her teammate that she walked right into a glass door.

Although clumsy on land, Anne showed great poise in the water, winning a gold medal in the 200-metre and silver in the 100-metre breaststroke at those Commonwealth Games. That same year, she also won silver and bronze medals at the 1982 World Championships. During the 1983 Pan-American Games, Ottenbrite's powerful whip-kick cost her a medal. At the time, no part of the body was allowed out of the water, except for the swimmer's head and neck — officials felt that it would make the stroke too similar to a front crawl. Anne won the 200-metre race, but was later disqualified because her feet had broken the water's surface. The regulations have now changed and the whip-kick style that Ottenbrite pioneered is used today by many world champion breast-stroke swimmers. The next day, Anne adjusted her stroke so that her feet remained in the water and she went on to win the 100-metre breaststroke gold medal at the same competition. In total, Ottenbrite had set eight national and three Commonwealth games records. By 1984, Anne Ottenbrite had established herself as one of the top threats for a gold medal at the Los Angeles Olympic Games.

But two months before the Olympic Games, on May 21, 1984, Anne's clumsiness put her chances for an Olympic medal in jeopardy. While getting ready for a night out in Montreal, Ottenbrite lifted her left leg to show her friend that the deck shoes she was wearing were likely inappropriate for night clubs. But when she lifted her leg, she heard a horrifying popping sound — she looked down to find her other knee sliding out of place. She fainted. Anne was rushed to the hospital, her knee was put into a brace, and she was given crutches. While Ottenbrite continued to train with the team, she worried that her Olympic dream would have to wait four more years. The injury to her knee meant she couldn't use her extraordinary whip-kick because the hard, fast, circular motion put too much pressure on her knee.

Even though doctors predicted she might be healed enough in time to compete in the Olympics, she wouldn't be able to compete in the Olympic team trials being held only four weeks after her accident. Her knee would not be strong enough to withstand the pressure of her powerful whip-kick. But the team's head coach, Trevor Tiffany, knew that Anne stood a good chance to win a medal if she could get to the Olympics, so he made the unprecedented decision to include Ottenbrite on the Olympic team even though she did not truly qualify. Anne left for Los Angeles, still wearing the brace on her knee.

Only a week before the heats were to begin for the 200-metre breast-stroke, Anne's specialty, she felt that her knee had healed and she practised without a brace for the first time since the injury. But even in Los Angeles,

Anne was at risk of freak accidents. Just days before the competition, the team's bus was hit from behind. Anne was sitting in the only frontward facing seat and suffered whiplash as a result. She also managed to pull her groin during a workout. Despite this string of unfortunate luck, Anne was able to put all the freak injuries behind her when she dived from her starting block for the first 200-metre heat. Though her arm caught the water while surfacing, costing her precious seconds, she still qualified for the final by less than three-tenths of a second.

Warming up for the final, Anne saw that her Canadian teammate, Alex Baumann, had won the individual medley competition in swimming. When Anne heard her country's national anthem being played as Baumann was awarded the gold medal she was inspired. She swam the first half of the 200-metre final at world record pace. Though her pace slowed slightly during the last half, it was fast enough to beat all other competitors. Anne Ottenbrite won Canada's first gold medal in female swimming at an Olympic Games.

Though she was thrilled with her victory, Ottenbrite was determined to return home with more than one medal. For the 100-metre final, she had a terrible start and was in last place at the 75-metre mark, but gave an all-out sprint during the last 25 metres to capture the silver medal. She would also add a bronze medal to her collection by swimming the breast-stroke segment of the Canadian team relay.

Anne attended the University of Southern California that fall on a swimming scholarship, but she transferred to Wilfred Laurier University in Waterloo, Ontario, after her second year. She formally retired from competitive swimming at age 20, but soon discovered a new passion — coaching. She has since coached swimming at the Burlington Aquatic Club, Region of Waterloo Swim Club, Guelph University and at the Pickering Swim Club.

Anne Ottenbrite was inducted into the Swim Ontario Hall of Fame, the International Swimming Hall of Fame and the Canadian Sports Hall of Fame for her many athletic achievements. She has also been named a Companion of the Order of Canada. The water has also played a part in her personal life; she met her husband, Marlin Muylaert, a professional hockey coach, at a pool party. They have two children.

Despite a serious accident weeks before the 1984 Games in Los Angeles, Ottenbrite recovered to become the first Canadian woman ever to win a gold medal in swimming.

In addition to being a medal winner, Anne Ottenbrite was a pioneer in the world of competitive swimming. The whip-kick technique that she developed is now used by many world champion breaststroke swimmers. Anne was plagued with a clumsiness on land that almost cost her the chance to compete for gold in the water. But her own fierce determination and a head coach's courage to break with tradition resulted in three Olympic medals.

"SHE'S A REAL COMPETITOR,
DETERMINED TO WIN AT ANY COST."

JIM THOMPSON, IRENE MacDONALD'S FIRST COACH

IRENE
MacDONALD

Diving through the Pain

IRENE MacDONALD WAS DENIED a chance to compete in the Olympics in 1952 because of the Canadian team's lack of funds. When she arrived at the 1956 Summer Games in Melbourne, Australia, she was determined to win an Olympic medal. She finished the women's springboard diving preliminary round of competition in second place and was well on her way to a silver medal. On her second dive of the finals, she walked on to the springboard and prepared for her dive. When she attempted to lift her arm, an intense pain shot through her shoulder. It was so severe that she couldn't complete her dive. Instead, she retreated from the diving board in tears. MacDonald had her arm frozen by an anesthetic and regained her composure. Despite the pain in her arm, she returned to complete her final dives. With determination and focus, Irene captured a bronze medal — the first medal in aquatic sports ever won by a Canadian woman.

Born in Hamilton, Ontario, on November 22, 1933, Irene MacDonald spent most of her youth in an orphanage. When she was 13, Irene was introduced to aquatic sports when she escorted another girl from the orphanage to the city pool in Hamilton. The swimmer's coach, Jack McCormick, convinced Irene to get into the water as well. And soon it was

Irene MacDonald soars through the air en route to capturing Canada's first Olympic medal in women's diving at the 1956 Melbourne Olympic Games.

At the age of seventeen, Irene MacDonald (right) became the Canadian springboard diving champion. She won the title a total of 15 times before she retired.

hard to get her out. Irene felt a comfort in the pool that she couldn't find anywhere else. The water was a refuge for the troubled teenager; a place where she could escape from feelings of inadequacy and low self-esteem. Irene felt ashamed to be an orphan and she was troubled by her appearance. She had crooked teeth and terrible acne throughout her teenage years. But she excelled in the pool, and she quickly gained both experience and confidence. MacDonald first became a competitive swimmer and then switched to diving. By 1951, at the age of 17, Irene MacDonald became the Canadian springboard diving champion. She would win the Canadian Championship 15 times before finally retiring from the sport.

Shortly after she won her first Canadian title, MacDonald moved to Kelowna, British Columbia, to train under Dr. George Athans Sr.

Dr. Athans felt that Irene showed enormous promise — and he was correct in his assessment. Irene won a place on the 1952 Canadian Olympic team as its top female diver, but tragically, the team had to drop a number of athletes weeks before the Games because of a lack of funds. Irene MacDonald would have to wait four more years for a chance at the Olympics. In 1954, the slight, 110-pound, five-foot two-inch athlete attained her first international success by winning the bronze medal at the British Empire and Commonwealth Games (now the Commonwealth Games) held in Vancouver. Irene was small, fast, and able to complete tight twists and spins and then land with her body in near perfect vertical formation. In addition to her natural ability, MacDonald had the determination to win. She practised for hours each day and worked whatever job necessary from secretary to stenographer to pay for coaching and practice time in the pool.

In late 1955, MacDonald realized that if she wanted to win an Olympic medal, she would have to train with the strong American team. They dominated the sport of diving — they had won 20 of the 21 Olympic medals presented in women's springboard diving from 1920 to 1952. MacDonald moved to Los Angeles to live with Pat McCormick, the American favourite for the gold medal, and Pat's husband, the coach of the U.S. women's diving team, Glenn McCormick. The long 10- to 12-hour days of training paid quick dividends — MacDonald finished second only to Pat McCormick in the U.S. national springboard championships. Rumours even circulated that Glenn McCormick tried to convince Irene to take U.S. citizenship and join the American team. But Irene MacDonald chose to represent her native Canada at the 1956 Melbourne Olympic Games.

Irene MacDonald proved her ability early in the competition by finishing the Olympic qualifying round in second place, only three points behind Pat McCormick. In her two final dives of the preliminary round, she received the highest marks of the day and the loudest support from the crowd. However, only she and her coach knew that MacDonald was suffering from a terrible case of bursitis in her shoulder, a condition that causes friction between the bone and muscle joint. Bursitis causes a healthy bursa sac to become inflamed; instead of gliding smoothly

Irene MacDonald with fellow Canadian athletes at the 1958 British Empire Commonwealth Games.

over the bone and muscles, it becomes gritty and rough. Every time MacDonald moved her shoulder or raised her arms, she would be subjected to throbbing pain. It was even more severe when she had to pull her shoulders and body tight to make a clean, splash-free, hands-first entry into the water.

During her second jump of the four-dive final, MacDonald walked out to the end of the springboard and tried to raise her arm in preparation for her dive. But the pain in her shoulder had finally become too debilitating. MacDonald stopped and walked off the board crying. Trainers froze her arm with an anesthetic and MacDonald decided to continue the competition. Unfortunately, according to the rules of competitive diving, when a diver has indicated that she is ready to begin a dive by stepping on the board, and then retreats from the diving board, she receives a penalty of six points. MacDonald, fighting back the tears and pushing through her pain, finished the competition with two strong dives. Her combined score of 121.40 was more than 20 points behind the leader, McCormick, but only four points behind the silver medalist,

American Jeanne Stunyo. Irene MacDonald had captured a bronze medal — the first medal won by a Canadian woman in any aquatic event. Had she not balked on her second attempt, MacDonald would have finished ahead of Stunyo and won the silver medal.

Irene MacDonald continued to compete for many years after the Melbourne Games. She came second in the 1958 British Empire and Commonwealth Games, for which she was named Canadian female athlete of the year. She also won six U.S. national championships, and she was selected for the Canadian Olympic team again in 1960. In Rome, MacDonald led the competition after six dives, but she let nerves get the best of her, made a costly error and finished in sixth place. MacDonald later suffered a detached retina and was forced to retire from diving.

After her final Olympic competition in 1960, Irene MacDonald played an instrumental role in helping Diving Canada form its own independent association. It had previously been part of the same governing body as swimming. MacDonald became a coach to numerous national champions and a broadcast commentator for the CBC. As a commentator, she covered diving events from the 1976 through to the 1988 Olympic Games. Remembering her own disappointment in not being able to compete at the 1952 Olympic Games, MacDonald also helped to support young Canadian divers. She personally funded numerous athletes and paid their expenses so that they could travel to international competitions. In the later stages of her life, MacDonald suffered from Alzheimer's disease and required the financial support of the community to live her final days in a rest home.

MacDonald was recognized for her distinguished career by earning a place in the B.C. Sports Hall of Fame, the Canadian Sports Hall of Fame, the Canadian Olympic Hall of Fame and the Canadian Aquatic Hall of Fame. She was also awarded the Order of British Columbia.

Irene MacDonald first took to the water for comfort, but she went on to gain confidence in all areas of her life through her many successes in springboard diving. Her many sacrifices and her conviction to excel at this sport made her Canadian champion in the 1950s and won her a place on the 1956 Canadian Olympic team. Her determination to compete despite excruciating pain in her shoulder resulted in a bronze medal and set the standard for competitive diving in Canada.

EGERTON
MARCUS

Broken Dream, Silver Lining

"Even with two broken hands, I'd have taken the fight. I came here to win the gold medal and couldn't possibly give up the opportunity."

EGERTON MARCUS

FOR MANY CANADIANS their most enduring memory of the 1988 Summer Olympics in Seoul is the elation and then embarrassment that surrounded Ben Johnson's gold medal run and the subsequent steroid scandal. The Games should instead be remembered for a Canadian boxer's stubborn refusal to let a broken hand deprive him of his dream. Powerful Canadian middleweight boxer Egerton Marcus broke his right hand during his third bout of the Olympic Games. With his most potent weapon broken and swelling in size, Marcus still managed to focus on his dream of an Olympic gold medal and fought through the pain. He won his next two fights, but ultimately lost the gold medal match. He returned home to Canada with a silver medal — a silver lining for his broken dream.

It was not surprising that Egerton Marcus chose boxing as both his sport and profession — it was in his family. Born in Guyana in 1965, Marcus immigrated to Toronto at a young age. His uncle, Charlie Arnos, represented Guyana in boxing at the 1968 Mexico Games and his mother was also a boxer. Marcus quickly became a stellar fighter. He was focused, in good shape, and he trained rigorously. He was quick, with excellent instincts and an ability to read his opponent. He also developed potent punch combinations. But it was particularly his power and strength

The powerful and determined Egerton Marcus (left) competes in the boxing event at the 1988 Olympic Games in Seoul.

that made him feared by his opponents. Even though amateur bouts last only three rounds and fighters wear protective headgear, Marcus still won the majority of his bouts by knockout. His speed allowed him to move in on his opponents and then nail them with vicious right hooks. During the late 1980s, he became the number one amateur middleweight boxer in Canada and was one of the top-ranked boxers in the world.

Heading into the 1988 Games in South Korea, the number one-ranked amateur middleweight fighter in the world was Angel Espinoza of Cuba. But Espinoza would not compete at the Olympics, because the Cuban government decided to stand united with North Korea and boycott the Games. This left Egerton Marcus as one of the top prospects for a gold medal. Before the 1988 Olympic Games, *Sports Illustrated* predicted that Marcus, along with the taller East German fighter Henry Maske, would be in contention for a medal and could challenge for Olympic gold.

Thirty-four boxers were scheduled to compete for the middleweight medals. Egerton Marcus needed to beat five challengers to make it to the gold medal bout. During his third fight at the Olympics, the right-handed Canadian knocked out Yugoslavia's Darko Dukic in the second round with a vicious right cross, but the hit had serious consequences. Marcus suffered one of the worst injuries imaginable for a boxer: he broke his right hand. This was not an unfamiliar injury to him — he had missed the 1987 Pan-Am games because of a broken right hand. With unfailing resolve, Egerton Marcus decided he would not let his dream of Olympic gold die, no matter what damage it might do to his future professional boxing career. Egerton Marcus chose to fight with his knuckle separated and his hand so swollen that it was virtually round. He forced smiles when doctors examined his hand after each fight. Egerton was not even allowed the usual luxury of pain killers for fear of being caught doping. Instead Egerton Marcus chose to fight.

Even with a broken right hand, Egerton Marcus won his next two fights and reached the gold medal bout against the number one-ranked amateur boxer, Henry Maske of East Germany. Like much of the boxing world, Maske knew about Marcus' broken hand and planned his strategy accordingly. Marcus' trainer, Adrian Teodorescu, decided that Marcus would have to throw a lot of rights early to catch the East German by surprise and possibly knock him out. Marcus followed Teodorescu's strategy. His daring right-handed attack not only took the East German by surprise, but also put genuine fear in the boxer's eyes as he tried to dodge Marcus' vicious rights. Unfortunately, although stunned and hurt, Maske survived Marcus' flurry; he didn't fall. But that series of rights had taken its toll. The pain in Marcus' right hand grew unbearable. In the next minute, everyone knew the fight was over. Egerton was unable to throw a right without grimacing in terrible pain. With sheer grit and determination, Marcus held out the full three rounds, hoping that his strong first round performance would be enough to convince the judges of his victory. It wasn't. Henry Maske won by unanimous decision.

When the fight was over, Egerton did not complain about the circumstances; instead he apologized to the people of Canada. "I want to tell the people of Canada how sorry I am that I couldn't do it for them."

After the 1988 Olympics, Marcus relinquished his amateur status to fight professionally. He switched weight classes and successfully won the North American Boxing Federation's light heavyweight belt in 1992 and '93, despite continuous fracturing of his right hand. In February 1995, he was given a chance to avenge his Olympic loss when he faced Henry Maske in Frankfurt, Germany, for the International Boxing Federation's light heavyweight title. Marcus lost again, this time by a 12-round unanimous decision.

Egerton Marcus is still boxing professionally at age 38. His professional record is 16 wins, 13 by knockout, four losses and one draw. His main role now is not as contender, but as coach to his cousin, Troy Ross, another former Canadian Olympic boxer and light heavyweight contender.

Because of his courage and determination, Egerton Marcus' Olympic dream of a gold medal was not lost, but replaced with silver. He showed that a fighter's heart could be as important as his hands in winning bouts and attaining Olympic glory.

Chapter Four

OF
PRINCIPLES

"THREE YEARS EARLIER, NO ONE HAD REALLY LISTENED TO ME WHEN I SAID THE NAZIS WERE BAD GUYS. NOW THEY WERE GOING TO SPEND THE NEXT FIVE-AND-A-HALF YEARS FIGHTING THEM."

SAMMY LUFTSPRING, *CALL ME SAMMY*

SAMMY
LUFTSPRING

Sitting Out to Speak Out

IN 1936, Sammy Luftspring, then one of Canada's top-ranked amateur boxers, would make one of the most important decisions of his career, to speak out against the evils he saw in Hitler's Germany by boycotting the 1936 Berlin Olympic Games.

Luftspring was the son of Jewish immigrants from Slipia, Poland. He grew up in the Jewish ghetto of Toronto's Kensington Market during the Prohibition-era 1920s. Though his father was a practising Orthodox Jew, Sam found little to interest him in religion. Instead, Sammy turned his devotion to another subject — boxing. He got his first taste for boxing at the age of 10 when his father took him to an amateur bout at the Standard Theatre in Toronto. The actual event did not impress him as much as the star treatment that the victor received. The winner of the bout was paraded down the streets of Kensington Market. Sammy wanted that same glory and admiration for himself.

Shortly thereafter, Sam took up boxing. He trained every spare moment he could find and spent much of his money on matinee showings of "fight pictures" to learn proper ring craft. Luftspring soon discovered that his greatest strengths were speed and instincts. In his autobiography, *Call Me Sammy*, he said, "I got into fighting because I discovered I could easily

Sammy Luftspring fought with a Star of David on his trunks as a reminder of his Jewish heritage.

avoid being hit." Throughout his youth, he mastered the technique known as counterpunching. Sam would draw his opponents to throw punches at him which he would block or avoid, and then he would counter with a solid punch of his own. A good counterpuncher will land many more punches than his adversary because his opponent often leaves either his body or his face unprotected when he throws the first punch. Sam would frequently stun and often knock out his opponents by catching them off balance when his counterpunches connected.

With this technique, his inherent ability and admirable discipline, Sammy Luftspring became the amateur welterweight champion of Ontario in 1935. He went on to become one of the top-ranked amateur boxers in the country. As it has been for so many legendary boxers, the Summer Olympic Games would have been his final amateur triumph and a chance to earn an international reputation before he turned professional.

In 1936, Luftspring had defeated all challengers in the Canadian Championships in Edmonton with the exception of a contested decision won by Robin Carrington of Alberta. But it was not the decision in the bout against Carrington that kept Luftspring from the 1936 Berlin Olympic Games; he was still Canada's best hope for a medal in the welterweight division. Sammy Luftspring sacrificed his ambition for something more important — his self-respect. He decided not to attend the Games as an act of protest against the Nazi regime's treatment of Jews and other minorities. By doing so, Sammy also gave up the opportunity to face the world's best amateur boxers and prove his talent. As Luftspring admitted many times over his career, he relished the fame and publicity of being a boxer. Giving up the opportunity to build an international fan base and gain Canadian glory was a big sacrifice.

Luftspring also felt that Canadian Jewish athletes should show solidarity, so he convinced another top Jewish Canadian amateur boxer, "Baby" Yack, to withdraw from the Canadian Olympic trials. On July 7, 1936, Sammy wrote to Canada's major newspapers on behalf of Yack and himself to explain to Canadians why the two boxers had made their decision not to attend the Games.

"We desire to advise you that we have decided not to take part in the boxing trials to be held in Montreal to select the Canadian Olympic team,"

"FOR EVERY ROUND OF THE DAY,
I WEAR AN ADAM HAT"

SAMMY LUFTSPRING

WELTERWEIGHT CHAMPION
OF CANADA

COSMOPOLITAN

*Boxing legend Sammy Luftspring was Canadian welterweight champion for three years
before he suffered an eye injury in 1940 that ended his career.*

Luftspring wrote. "It is a matter of keen disappointment to us to turn down the opportunity of trying for the great honor and privilege of making a place on the Canadian team. However, we have gone into the community, and find that we cannot act differently from what we have decided. We know that we, as Canadian boys, would be personally safe, and perhaps well received in Germany. But can we forget the way the German government is treating the Jewish boys in Germany? The German government is treating our brothers and sisters worse than dogs. Can Canadian sportsmen blame us for refusing to take part in a meet sponsored by people who would humiliate and degrade and persecute us too, if we did not happen to have the great fortune of being Canadians? We are making a personal sacrifice in refusing the chance and we are sure that all true Canadian sportsmen will appreciate that we would have been very low to hurt the feelings of our fellow Jews by going to a land that would exterminate them if it could. We wish the Canadian team every success."

Unfortunately, few other athletes followed their example. The 1936 Summer Olympic Games in Berlin came to be known as the Olympics that brought amateur sport into the modern era. In the 1932 Games in Los Angeles, 1,408 athletes from 37 nations competed. In the 1936 Berlin Games, the number of participants nearly tripled to 4,066 athletes from 49 nations. The United States and Canada both sent their largest athletic contingents. The Games became a propaganda vehicle for the Nazi regime. The world watched as German athletes were awarded the most medals by a wide margin. Sammy Luftspring's warning to the Canadian people would soon prove prophetic — Canada declared war on Germany three years later.

In the years after the Games, Sammy Luftspring proved that had he competed in Berlin, he would likely have returned home with a medal. He turned professional late in 1936. Less than two years later, he became Canadian welterweight champion and held the title for two years. In 1940, Luftspring was the third-ranked welterweight boxer in the world and had a contract in hand to face the world champion, Henry Armstrong, when tragedy struck. During the first round of the fight preceding his scheduled World Championship bout, his opponent, Steve Belloise, caught Sammy in the left eye with his thumb. Even though his left eye closed,

Sammy continued to fight and took a serious pounding from Belloise, especially on his damaged eye. As a result, Sammy suffered a torn retina — an injury that left him blind in his left eye and ended his boxing career at age 24.

Luftspring would later return to the ring as a referee, and he earned a place in the *Guinness Book of World Records* for refereeing 2,000 boxing matches. He was the only referee ever to return a fighter's punch. In 1985, the principled Luftspring was inducted into the Canadian Sports Hall of Fame.

BECKIE
SCOTT

Drug-Free

"I still believe that there are clean athletes who are successful and can reach the top, regardless of the doping that goes on. I have to."

BECKIE SCOTT, 2001

BECKIE SCOTT is a trailblazer in the sport of cross country skiing in Canada and the world. On the trails, Scott has posted some of the country's best-ever results in women's cross-country skiing. And she has done so despite the fact that her competition has long held an unfair advantage — Scott is a clean athlete in a sport where illegal doping is rampant. Before the 2002 Salt Lake City Olympic Games, Beckie Scott started a petition to pressure international cross-country officials to acknowledge the problem and take action. Initially, her efforts appeared to be successful — the World Anti-Doping Agency took over drug testing for the International Ski Federation (FIS). But the results proved otherwise. Just days after Scott attained Canada's first-ever cross-country skiing Olympic medal, a bronze in the five-kilometre pursuit event, the two Russian women who took first and second in the race, Larissa Lazutina and Olga Danilova, were caught for doping.

Beckie Scott was born in Vermilion, Alberta, on August 1, 1974. It only seemed natural that she would become a cross-country skier — her family lived on the border of a national park with ski trails and her parents were avid cross-country skiers themselves. Scott put on her ski shoes, grabbed her poles and clicked into her skis for the first time at the

Cross-country skier Beckie Scott skis the fourth leg of the Women's 4-by-5-kilometre relay at the 2002 Winter Olympic Games in Salt Lake City.

age of five. Even though she was a serious and competitive skier, it was the social aspect of the sport that initially appealed to her. Beckie's mother started the Jack Rabbit Ski League, a kids' ski club, which gave Beckie many opportunities to meet and hang out with kids her own age while skiing. But during that time, she also developed a competitive drive and natural athletic ability that would make her a champion. By age 12, she was already winning medals at the junior level and she went on to make the national team in the mid 1990s.

Scott's steady progress and competitive placings on the World Cup circuit earned her the right to represent Canada at the 1998 Olympic Games in Nagano, Japan. Her results were typical of a Canadian team that had never won a medal in cross-country skiing and rarely had showings in the top 20. Scott finished 45th, 47th and 51st in her three races. Shortly after those Games, Beckie made the decision that she could and would do better. She moved to the United States to live and train with her boyfriend, now husband, Justin Wadsworth. She hired her own personal coach from the Norwegian team and also a personal trainer who encouraged her to incorporate her own feelings and ideas into her training. Under this new direction, Scott's performance improved. She began to capture numerous top 10 finishes in 1998, 1999 and 2000. In 2001, she received her first medal in a World Cup event in the 1.5-kilometre sprint at Soldier Hollow, U.S.A.

At these competitions, Scott learned of the prevalence of drug use in the sport. She had her suspicions in the late 1990s, but in 2001, her worst fears were confirmed. Six members of the Finnish team were caught using a blood-expanding product at the Lahti, Finland, World Championships. Not only did the European skiers have the advantages of better trails, better coaching and World Cup circuit races on home soil, many of them were also using artificial substances to enhance their performance. Scores of skiers were taking chemical agents that improved endurance by boosting the oxygen-carrying capacity of their blood. Beckie Scott and Justin Wadsworth began a petition that caught the attention of the International Ski Federation because it included signatures from 115 of the world's leading cross-country skiers and coaches.

The petition implored the FIS to acknowledge and take action against the drug-use problem.

Beckie Scott also set out to prove by example that drug-free athletes can achieve top results on the world circuit. She focused specifically on the Olympics in Salt Lake City. During the 2001 and 2002 seasons, Scott trained as often as she could on the trails at Soldier Hollow, the venue for the cross-country events at Salt Lake City. She was determined to learn all the nuances of the course: hills, ruts, where to hold back and the most opportune times to challenge, so that she would be the best technical skier. She also trained on high altitude courses as often as possible to simulate how her breathing would be affected in Salt Lake City. She even trained at night, sleeping in a tent to simulate the thin air at high altitudes to help her body acclimatize.

When the Games began in February 2002, Scott was expected to finish in the top 10 and possibly even contend for a medal. Her results in Salt Lake were extraordinary. In her first event, the 10 kilometre classic, she finished a surprising sixth — the best performance ever by a Canadian cross-country skier at an Olympic Games. In the 1.5-kilometre sprint competition, Beckie caught a couple of drafts and made a couple of tactical errors, allowing herself to be boxed in by other skiers. Because it was her strongest event, Beckie still managed to finish in fifth place. In the team relay, she earned another top 10 performance. Her team finished in eighth place and Beckie unofficially recorded the second best time of all skiers in the race.

Scott's best performance came in the middle of the Games in the five-kilometre pursuit event. Her aim was to hang in tight with the leading pack, but to keep enough energy in reserve to challenge for a medal at the finish. The two Russian skiers, Larissa Lazutina and Olga Danilova were given good start positions, which they never yielded. Scott paced herself with the next pack of skiers. With less than 500 metres remaining, Beckie made her move to pass the other skiers in her pack and put herself into third place. But during the course's final hill, Katerina Neumannova of the Czech Republic closed in and passed Beckie. Scott summoned everything she had and battled back. The two skiers stayed neck-and-neck to the finish, so close, in fact, that a photo finish was required to determine who would take home the bronze medal. Photos revealed that Scott's ski crossed the line about fifteen centimetres ahead of Neumannova's — Beckie Scott was awarded the bronze medal.

Shortly after her medal-winning performance, Beckie was in the spotlight again. This time it was not so much for her incredible achievements, but for her role in the anti-doping campaign. In subsequent races, both Russian skiers Lazutina and Danilova tested positive for the performance-enhancing drug darbepoetin. Appeals from the Canadian Olympic Association, the World Anti-Doping Agency and the Norwegian Olympic Committee were successful. Lazutina belatedly declared to have doped in her December 2001 races and therefore should not have been eligible to compete in the Salt Lake Games — she was stripped of her silver medal. On December 18, 2003, The Court of Arbitration for Sport ruled that Olga Danilova also be stripped of her gold medal. Nearly twenty-two months after the close of the Salt Lake City Games, Beckie Scott was finally awarded the gold medal she deserved for her championship performance.

Evidence from a recent study by Doctors Stray-Gundersen and Videman of the University of Alberta verify that drug use is rampant in the international world of cross-country skiing. Their analysis of blood samples from the 2001 World Championships at Lahti, Finland, demonstrated that "as many as 50 percent of the World Championship medalists and one in three top-10 finishers engaged in some form of blood doping" (Christie, *the Globe and Mail*). Scott remains optimistic that actions can be taken to discourage and deter drug use. Though it was her campaign that brought the doping issue to light, Scott is grounded in the reality that much of the responsibility lies with the International Ski Federation. Until the governing body takes action to eliminate doping, it will likely remain a problem, leaving the clean skiers like herself at a competitive disadvantage.

Despite this inherent disadvantage, Scott also believes that drug-free skiers can still achieve top results. Beckie still competes in cross-country skiing. She finished ninth in the World Cup standings in 2003 and is now taking competition one year at a time.

Beckie Scott receives the bronze medal for the women's 5-kilometre Free Pursuit at the 2002 Olympic Winter Games in Salt Lake City. Her medal was later upgraded to gold when Lazutina and Danilova were stripped of their medals for doping.

In the summer of 2003, she married her long-time boyfriend and member of the U.S. cross-country team, Justin Wadsworth. When not training or racing, Beckie keeps busy with her many speaking engagements, including the many "Beckie Scott Days" held throughout Canada to celebrate her accomplishments and to coincide with outdoor winter activities. She is also working on her English degree through correspondence at the University of Waterloo. Beckie's other priority is that of a special representative for Canada with UNICEF. During 2003, she travelled to West Africa with the United Nations organization and hopes to continue to work with UNICEF to benefit children worldwide.

Beckie Scott has broken ground in women's nordic sports in Canada and the world — both on and off the trails. Her petition and lobbying have brought to light the extent of the drug-use problem in cross-country skiing. While the situation will not be improved until the sport's governing body, the FIS, takes action, Scott's performance in Salt Lake City proved that North American skiers can compete effectively against their European counterparts and that drug-free athletes can win medals.

Chapter Five

INNOVATORS

THE
MATCHLESS SIX
Role Challengers & Record Breakers

"It didn't make any difference if we were the first women or not.
We were there to compete and win. That was the main thing."

ETHEL SMITH, SPRINTER

FROM JULY 30 to August 5, 1928, in Amsterdam, Netherlands, six Canadians not only became the first women to compete in track-and-field at the Olympic Games, they also emerged as heroes by winning more medals — two gold, a silver and a bronze — and collecting more points than any other team.

In the early 1920s, women were discouraged from participating in international sporting events. It was considered immoral and overtly masculine for women to run, jump and exert themselves in public com petition. It was further feared that these types of activities could harm a woman's reproductive organs. Nevertheless, by the end of World War I many women began challenging these ideas by participating in sports through school or company teams. Track-and-field, however, remained mostly a sport for male athletes. The only competitive events for women were loosely organized running races at company picnics. That would change forever with the success of Canada's female athletes in track-and-field in Amsterdam in 1928.

When the Olympics were reintroduced in 1896 in Athens, organizers wanted to be true to the ancient Greek games, which meant only men could compete. Baron Pierre de Coubertin, considered the founder of

The Matchless Six: (top row) Ethel Smith, Jean Thompson, (middle row) Ethel Catherwood, Jane Bell, (bottom row) Bobbie Rosenfeld, Myrtle Cook. These six Canadian women dominated women's track and field at the 1928 Summer Olympic Games in Amsterdam.

the modern Olympics, was "personally against the participation of women in public competitions" according to historian Ron Hotchkiss. Organizers felt that women should exercise for their own health, but were strongly opposed to letting women participate in organized competitions and immoral and scandalous public displays.

The driving force behind the women's sports movement post World War I was La Fédération des Sociétés Féminines Sportives de France, which evolved into the Fédération Sportive Féminine Internationale (FSFI) in 1921. Alice Milliat, the federation's leader for most of its existence, had a two-pronged approach to legitimizing organized women's athletic competitions. First, she would petition the International Olympic Committee to introduce events for female competitors. Then, in their absence, she would hold her own Olympic competitions.

Her plan proved successful, as the International Amateur Athletic Federation (IAAF) parties agreed to include a limited number of female events in the 1924 Olympic Games, and then agreed to introduce women's track-and-field at the 1928 Games. There would be only five track events offered and only as an experiment. Women were going to have to prove their ability and popularity with the spectators to make women's track-and-field competition a mainstay at the Olympic Games.

Meanwhile, in Canada, the first formal competition for women was held in 1923 at the Canadian National Exhibition's Athletic Day in Toronto. Organizers wanted to capitalize on the popularity of sports competitions, so they held the event on the last day of the exhibition. To increase the audience, they also decided to invite a group of well-established women runners from Chicago. Since Canada offered no recognized running competitions for women, Hughes had to seek out unheralded novices with ability to compete. The team he selected, two of whom, Myrtle Cook and Bobbie Rosenfeld, would later represent Canada at the 1928 Olympics, defeated the Americans. Canadian women runners soon began to make a name for themselves by competing, winning and setting world records in North American track meets.

Before the 1928 Canadian Olympic trials in Halifax, the Canadian Olympic Association was determined that it was going to send a team of six women to compete in the five track events. Some countries would

Bobbie Rosenfeld wears her Patterson Chocolate Company track uniform. She was chosen by the Canadian Press as the Female Athlete of the First Half Century (1901 to 1950).

send women's teams with as many as 19 members. There would be four members for the four-by-100-metre relay, all of whom would also compete in the 100-metre sprint; one woman to compete in a field event, either discus or high jump; and one alternate, who could possibly compete in the 800-metre. When the trials were over, three world and five Canadian records had been set. The Canadian women's team had established itself as the squad to beat.

Myrtle Cook was a legal secretary from Toronto. Based on her experience, she was selected as the unofficial captain. She had participated in sports since she was 12 and had a natural ability and consuming desire to win. She was the world record holder in the 100-metre sprint, director of athletics for Toronto's Canadian Ladies Athletic Club, and she coached women runners. Winning at the Olympics was so important to her that she chose to postpone her wedding until after the Games.

Ethel Smith was also from Toronto. Her family didn't have much money and Ethel was forced to leave school at age 14 to work at an embroidery company. Sports, particularly running, were at first her escape from work and then became her passion. She joined a track-and-field team sponsored by the local hydro commission and then became a member of the Canadian Ladies Athletic Club. Her training, as for most of the other women, was rudimentary; it consisted simply of straight running and rubdowns. After securing a place on the team by placing second in the 100-metre sprint at the Halifax trials, she too decided to postpone her wedding until after the Games so she could concentrate on her training.

Fanny "Bobbie" Rosenfeld immigrated to Canada from Dneipropetrovsk, Russia, in 1905. She was a factory worker at the Patterson Chocolate Company. She was also a natural athlete. In addition to track-and-field, she excelled at tennis, softball, basketball and hockey. At a community picnic in Beaverton, Ontario, Rosenfeld was persuaded to run in the 100-yard dash. She won, beating the Canadian champion. At the 1925 Ontario Ladies Track-and-field Championship, she single-handedly won the points total for the Pats Athletic Club by placing first in the discus, shot put, 220- and 120-yard hurdles and the running long jump; and placing second in the 100-yard dash and javelin. She was selected to the team mainly for her abilities in the discus (she had set a

Canadian record at the Halifax trials); her running abilities were simply additional assets.

At 17, Jean Thompson was the youngest member of the team. One of her high school teachers, L.A. Wendling, noticed her ability and decided to be her personal coach. Thompson trained by running alongside Wendling's car as he shouted instructions and by running the bases with the local men's baseball team. She was so popular in her hometown of Penetanguishene, Ontario, that the town paid for her trip to the Halifax trials. She won a spot on the team by setting a new world record in the 800-metre with a time of 2:21.80 seconds.

Ethel Catherwood was born in North Dakota, U.S.A., but grew up in Scott, Saskatchewan. She excelled at numerous sports and had a natural ability for the high jump. When she moved to Saskatoon in 1925 and jumped over five feet, at a high school track meet, she attracted the attention of Joe Griffiths, the head of the physical education department at the University of Saskatchewan. Griffiths constructed a high jump pit near the back of Catherwood's house and worked with the high jumper on improving her style. By 1926 she had set an unofficial record in the high jump in a Regina provincial meet. When she set a new world record of five feet two inches at the Canadian National Exhibition in Toronto, reporters took notice of both her ability and beauty, dubbing her "The Saskatoon Lily." At the Halifax trials, she set a new world record of five feet three inches to clinch her spot on the squad.

Jane Bell was a star athlete at Toronto's Central High School of Commerce, where she was a member of the swim and basketball teams and anchored the track team. Her training intensified and her performance in track events improved substantially after she joined the Parkdale Athletic Club and began training under coach Walter Knox, an ex-Olympic athlete himself. By focusing on style, strength and mental conditioning, Bell developed into an excellent sprinter and hurdler. Her speed and her skills turning the corners in sprints assured her the third leg on the four-by-100 team and the final spot on the Canadian women's Olympic team.

The first women's event at the Amsterdam Games was the 100-metre sprint. Strong performances by the Canadian women, Myrtle Cook, Ethel Smith and Bobbie Rosenfeld, secured them three of the six spots in the final.

Ethel Catherwood was already a world-record holder in high jump when she cleared 1.59 metres in Amsterdam.

To run in the 100-metre final, Rosenfeld had to give up her opportunity to compete in the discus as both events were held at the same time. The race had its share of drama with three false starts that led to the disqualification of Schmidt from Germany and Cook. The Canadian sat on the sidelines crying during the race. When the women executed their fourth start, Betty Robinson of the United States got off to an early lead. Rosenfeld caught up to her by the finish, and the two runners crossed the line in a dead heat. Since modern radar technology had not yet been invented, the winner was determined by two judges, one to pick the winner, the other to pick the runner-up. Both judges picked Robinson. The chief judge, an American, made the final decision: Betty Robinson was awarded the gold medal, Bobbie Rosenfeld the silver and Ethel Smith the bronze. Most Canadian officials disagreed with the decision and tried to lodge a formal protest. Unfortunately, one key Canadian did not support the appeal — Dr. A.S. Lamb, head of the Canadian Olympic Committee. Many sports historians argue that Lamb's action was the main reason why the appeal was disallowed.

The 800-metre final was the next event for the Canadians. Jean Thompson, nursing a leg injury that she had suffered while training in Amsterdam, was the best hope, but Bobbie Rosenfeld had also qualified even though she had never trained for the event. The Canadian team decided to enter Rosenfeld in the event mainly to provide moral support to Thompson.

The 800-metre is a mid-distance race consisting of two full laps of the 400 metre track. Thompson started well and was in second place at the halfway point, but during the second lap she was quickly passed by other runners and dropped back to fourth place. Near the last half lap, Thompson decided to challenge, but so did the Japanese runner, Hitomi, who was running in fifth place. In passing Thompson, Hitomi jostled her, potentially further damaging Thompson's leg and pushing her out of the medals back into fourth place. Rosenfeld, who was running at the back of the pack, saw this and accelerated to pull even with Thompson. She cheered Thompson on for the last 30 metres to a fourth place finish and took fifth place herself. Many journalists, coaches and competitors have subsequently argued that Rosenfeld, who had so much endurance left to pull up from ninth to fifth place in less than 100 metres, likely could have challenged for a medal. Instead, she chose to focus on her teammate. According to historian Ron Hotchkiss, Canadian official Gibb remarked, "Bobbie Rosenfeld's sportsmanship in this event was one of the high spots of the games."

With three runners making the final in the 100-metre sprint, the Canadians were considered the strongest team for the four-by-100 relay. But the event also required good cornering skills and clean, quick hand-offs of the baton to ensure victory. The Canadian women had good fortune even before the race began, winning the coin toss and the strategic inside lane placement. Bobbie Rosenfeld was chosen to start, with Smith second, Jane Bell, who had a bandaged leg, running third and Cook running as the anchor, ready to avenge her disqualification in the 100-metre final. When Rosenfeld false-started, the Canadian team became edgy and apprehensive. The second start was clean. The Canadians finished the first leg of the race a close second to the U.S. team. Smith continued to keep pace with the Americans. When she handed off to Bell, the Canadians were still slightly behind in second place. Bell ran with great determination. By the time she finished her leg, she had moved nearly three metres ahead of the Americans. But the team's final hand-off was a harrowing experience. The rules require that a baton must be received cleanly by the next runner in the acceleration zone or the team is disqualified. As Bell was approaching the hand-off area, Cook broke into a sprint in the acceleration zone. Cook's pace was nearly too quick for Bell, who caught up to her only in the last few metres. With the baton in hand, Cook sped to the finish line, winning the race for the team and setting a world record of 48.40 seconds.

This would not be the last gold medal for the Canadians that day. The final event in women's track-and-field was the high jump. Ethel Catherwood, the world's record holder, was the favourite. She was also the fans' favourite. Her extraordinary beauty made her the most photographed woman athlete at the Games, and rumours abounded that a Hollywood career would follow. As was her custom, Catherwood began jumping in her sweat suit. She would leave it on until she missed an attempt. She and two other jumpers had cleared five feet and proceeded to five feet one inch. All of the competitors missed on their first attempt, including Catherwood. Before her next attempt, Ethel removed her sweat suit and then cleared the height; the other jumpers did not. The gold was hers.

Of the nearly 300 female athletes competing in the 1928 Olympic Games, the Canadian women finished the Olympics in first place with two gold medals, both won on the last day, in addition to the silver and bronze medals won earlier. When the women returned home to Canada, 200,000 fans greeted them with a parade and rally held in their honour.

The International Amateur Athletic Federation held a meeting on August 7, immediately following the women's competition. They decided by a vote of 16 to six to keep women's track-and-field events in the Olympic program, with the exception of the 800-metre race; it was still considered too strenuous for women. The Canadian people and the Canadian sports establishment, proud of the accomplishments of their Matchless Six, wanted to ensure that women would continue to compete and earn further Olympic glory.

After the Olympics, Myrtle Cook moved to Montreal, where she became a sportswriter for the *Montreal Star*. She married another sportswriter and had two children. She remained actively involved in the Canadian Olympic effort as well as amateur athletics. Ethel Smith married, divorced and lived the rest of her life in Toronto. Jean Thompson was convinced by her coach to stop running shortly after the Games. She married and raised a daughter. Jane Bell became a physical education director in Ontario, married and had two children. Ethel Catherwood never became an actress and retired from competitive sports in 1931. That same year she divorced and moved to California, where she became highly reclusive. Bobbie Rosenfeld was bed-ridden with arthritis within a year of the Games. She later became a sports columnist for *the Globe and Mail*. Despite her abruptly shortened career, the Canadian Press chose her as Canada's female athlete of the first half century primarily because of her accomplishments at the 1928 Olympic Games.

Canadian women have won numerous Olympic medals since the Amsterdam Summer Games, but the performance of these six women remains unmatched.

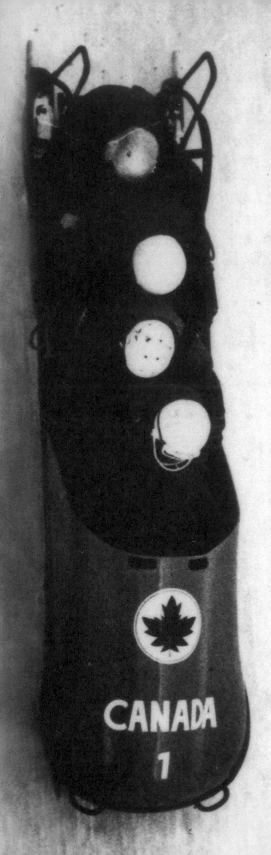

CANADA 1: 1964
BOBSLED TEAM

Thrill Seekers

"[It was] the greatest upset in bobsledding history."

U.S. BOBSLEDDER STAN BENHAM ON CANADA I

WHEN UNIVERSITY STUDENT Vic Emery read about a Canadian beating the world's tobogganing record on the 1.2-kilometre-long Cresta run in St. Moritz, Switzerland, he decided to try the run for a thrill, not realizing that this adventure would introduce him to his sporting obsession: the bobsled. Emery returned to Canada and, with his friend Lamont Gordon, founded the country's first bobsled club. He also recruited a number of adventurous fellow Canadians to join him in his devotion to the sport and in international competitions. Vic Emery and three of these recruits — his brother, John Emery, and friends Doug Anakin and Peter Kirby — would prove to the world that determination, sacrifice and focus could translate into Olympic glory.

Vic Emery grew up with a love for sports, developed largely from numerous summers spent swimming, canoeing and sailing with his brother at their cottage near Thunder Bay, Ontario. He was also an avid and competitive skier, but Vic Emery found his true sport passion in bob-sledding. In January 1956, Vic Emery was travelling across Europe with his fraternity brother Lamont Gordon when he got his first taste for high speed and high danger when they attempted the treacherous Cresta ice-toboggan run in St. Moritz, Switzerland. Shortly thereafter, Emery

Canada's pioneering bobsled team, composed of Doug Anakin, Vic Emery, John Emery and Peter Kirby, compete in a gold medal performance at the 1964 Innsbruck Winter Olympics.

The members of the Canada I team celebrate their hard-earned gold medal victory at the 1964 Innsbruck Winter Olympics.

hitched a ride with a group of British bobsledders to check out the Olympic Games in nearby Cortina d'Ampezzo, Italy. During that trip, Canadian bobsledding was born. Emery returned to Canada determined to become competitive in the sport, even though there was no Canadian bobsled sporting association, coaching, funds or course available for training.

With the support of Lieutenant Colonel George Machum and his friend, Lamont Gordon, Vic Emery formed the Laurentian Bobsledding Association. Even though he had a full-time job in Montreal as an engineer for an airline, Emery was determined to master the bobsled by centring much of his vacation time on trips to Europe to practise the sport. Emery and Gordon entered the 1959 World Championships in St. Moritz and recruited Vic's brother, John, and friend, Charles Rathgeb Jr., to complete the four-man bobsled team. The Canadians finished near last place in each of their three races and returned home with bumps and bruises from banging the corners of the course and even overturning their sled during one race. Nevertheless, the Canadian daredevils were determined to compete again.

The team struggled financially because the sport of bobsledding had no profile in Canada. They could not gain government support, nor much money from the community, and the young thrill seekers had little money of their own to support their newfound passion. In 1960, the United States could not build the 1,500-metre bobsled track for the Squaw Valley Olympic Games, so the bobsledding World Championships were held in Cortina d'Ampezzo, Italy. The poor Canadian team would not have been able to attend without the support of their friends on the Italian team who were keen to expand the field of bobsled competitors. The Italians paid for half of the Canadian team's airfare and lent them bobsleds.

According to the rules of international bobsledding competition, each team completes four runs. A team's final placement in the standings is based on its combined total time. In Italy, the Canadian team fared only slightly better than the previous year, finishing second to last in the four-man competition. The Canadians' combined time from their four runs was almost nine seconds off the leader, a substantial amount of time when considering that the differences between gold and silver is often only a few hundredths of a second.

Instead of being too discouraged with their poor showing, Emery's team returned to Canada determined to buy their own sleds and make the Canadians competitive. Emery's spirit was ignited by the thrill of charging down a manufactured 1.6-kilometre-long hill of ice at speeds of up to 150 kilometres an hour. He loved feeling the incredible gravitational force as the sled descended some 120 metres through the windy turns, and the rush of making split-second decisions on how to steer the sled based on instinct and feel. With Lamont Gordon, he went on an all-out campaign selling memberships in the club, asking friends and relatives for donations, and securing a loan to raise the necessary funds. Finally, during the 1961 World Championships, the team broke into the middle of the pack; it also learned firsthand the extreme danger of bobsledding.

In order to attain maximum speed, the driver needs to steer the sled in a perfectly straight line. This line needs to be high enough on the curves of the track to propel the sled faster, but low enough that the sled is not travelling extra distance. If the sled is too high, the risk of the sled shooting off course or overturning increases significantly. The course conditions can further increase the risk as the metal blades of the bob-sled can crack or stick in the melting ice. During the four-man event, one of the runners of Emery's sled (a metal strip underneath the sled that acts like a rudder to help guide it through the course) went through the ice, throwing it in the air. All of the riders were badly hurt and Vic narrowly escaped death as the sled landed just next to his helmet, smashing his nose.

Vic recovered from the accident with an even fiercer determination to improve. When bobsledding was first introduced as a competitive sport, it was thought that the heavier the crew, the greater the chance of success, since greater weight made for a faster run. The teams began in a seated position and were given a push start down the track. Crew members moved their bodies in a bobbing motion in an effort to propel the sled forward. When the running start was introduced, heavier crews were rarely able to deliver explosive starts. Sprint ability and strength became the most important elements: an advantage of one-hundredth of a second at the start translates into a gain of three-one-hundredths of a second or more at the end of the course. Consequently, Emery focused on recruiting strong Canadian athletes with good sprinting ability for his team. Three recruits in particular would be key to the team's success in 1964: John Emery, a standout sprinter in college, Peter Kirby, who had been a member of the Canadian ski team in the 1950s and Doug Anakin, a stocky athlete who had been a successful wrestler at university.

In 1962, the Canadians achieved their first real success. Although they did not have to compete against the top teams from Italy and Austria, they won a gold medal in the four-man competition at the Commonwealth Games. Their 1963 showing was not as impressive, but the team still managed to finish in the middle of the pack. If they were to compete for a medal at the Olympic Games at Innsbruck, they would need to shave off at least a second from each of their four runs.

With these thoughts in mind, eight men — Vic Emery, John Emery, Doug Anakin, Peter Kirby, Lamont Gordon, Chris Ondaatje, Gordon Currie and Dave Hobart — went to Europe with team manager Chuck Rathgeb Jr. and coach Doug Connor in January, 1964, for final training for the Olympic Games. When they arrived at Innsbruck, the Canadians were notified along with most other teams that the bobsled run was not

Canada's first bobsled team Doug Anakin, Vic Emery, John Emery and Peter Kirby, at the 1964 Innsbruck Winter Olympics.

open to foreign competitors, so they set off for Cortina d'Ampezzo to train. During their short stay in Italy, the Canadians tested alternative team combinations to ensure that they put themselves in the best position possible for the medals, even though they were considered a long shot. The four-man team would be Vic Emery, driver; Doug Anakin, number two; John Emery, number three; and Peter Kirby, brakeman. The brakeman became one of the most important members of the team. As the last man to enter the sled after the start, he needed to be the fastest and strongest sprinter on the team since he would be running for the longest time and would be giving the sled its final push. He also needed superior arm strength to slow the sled down at the end of the run by pulling hard on a lever attached to a saw-toothed brake that digs into the ice.

During their weeks of training, the Canadians significantly improved their starts by switching their footwear. At first, they wore football shoes, but found the spikes got stuck in the ice on warm days and provided little traction on cold days. The Canadians chose instead to use bowling shoes with strips of file cleaners glued to the soles. They also altered their start.

They decided to use a crouching start similar to when players line up at the line of scrimmage in football and then spring into a sprint. These changes, along with Vic Emery's improved driving ability, had immediate results. The team turned in some of the fastest practice times in Italy.

Back at Innsbruck, the two-man competition was one of the first events. Vic Emery and Peter Kirby narrowly missed the medals, finishing fourth. This strong showing convinced Emery that the Canadian four-man team could take home a medal. Because of uncertain weather conditions, the four-man competition was rescheduled one day in advance, which conflicted with the luge competition, in which Doug Anakin was competing. Vic convinced Anakin that his best chance for a medal was with the bobsled team. After the team's first run, Anakin knew he had made the right choice — Vic Emery's squad equalled the track record. At the end of the first day, after two runs, the Canadians were in first place with the two Italian teams in second and third. On the second day of competition, the Canadians had the second fastest run of the day and maintained their lead, but the Austrians had now moved into second place. The next morning was the final run. Emery and his team showed their resolve by posting the second fastest time of the day. In the process, they won Canada's only Olympic gold medal of the 1964 Winter Games and its first gold medal in bobsledding. The Canadian's team victory was decisive. They finished more than one second faster than the second place Austrians, with a combined total time of 4:14.46 versus 4:15.48. They had done the impossible. Even without government support, or a course to train on throughout the winter, they still took on the world and won.

The next year, Emery proved that the Canadian team's victory was no fluke as they took the World Championship for the first and only time. But with this glory attained and other more important life commitments that needed attention the team started to break up. Doug Anakin got married and felt that the sport was now too great a risk; Peter Kirby married, as well; John Emery, now a plastic surgeon, felt that he could not risk damage to his hands. After a Canadian sled crashed in 1966, killing one rider and leaving another unconscious, most of the other Canadian daredevils, including Vic Emery, agreed that it was time to retire.

Each member of that golden team enjoyed successful careers and started families after the Olympics. Vic Emery, now living in the U.K., became a wealthy businessman and father of three. He helped develop skiing and tourism in the Canadian Rockies. John Emery set up a plastic surgery practice in San Francisco, married and had two children. Doug Anakin retired from teaching and moved with his wife to British Columbia to live closer to his daughters and the great outdoors. Peter Kirby married, had two girls and started a ski equipment importing business in Quebec.

Vic Emery's search for high-speed thrills led him to the sport of bobsledding. His devotion, sacrifices and ingenuity along with that of his teammates led to the Canadian team's historic victory. Their golden Olympic story continues to motivate young Canadian bobsledders who dream of flying over the ice at breakneck speeds on their way to the Olympic podium.

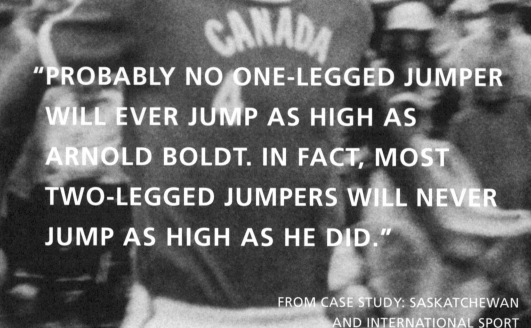

"PROBABLY NO ONE-LEGGED JUMPER WILL EVER JUMP AS HIGH AS ARNOLD BOLDT. IN FACT, MOST TWO-LEGGED JUMPERS WILL NEVER JUMP AS HIGH AS HE DID."

FROM CASE STUDY: SASKATCHEWAN AND INTERNATIONAL SPORT

ARNOLD
BOLDT

High Achiever

ARNOLD BOLDT lost his right leg in a farming accident before his third birthday. But that didn't stop him from competing in athletics. In addition to playing a variety of team sports, Arnold learned how to jump higher than any other disabled athlete and most able-bodied competitors. From leaping over cardboard boxes in his house to demonstrating high jump for the Pope, Boldt helped gain mainstream acceptance for disabled athletics. Boldt's determination, drive and dedication made him a true champion. During a 16 year period, Boldt completely dominated disabled athletics — he won five gold medals in the high jump at the Paralympic Games, as well as other medals for the long jump and volleyball.

Arnold Boldt was born on September 16, 1957, in Osler, Saskatchewan. When he was nearly three years old, he stepped into a grain auger. His right leg was mauled by the machine and had to be amputated above the knee. As a boy, Boldt decided that a missing limb wouldn't prevent him from being like all the other kids. He actively participated in many sports: soccer, hockey, softball, volleyball and track-and-field. He often played sports with his cousins, who worked hard and demanded that Arnold do the same. When he was in grades 4 through 6, Boldt's school hosted a

Arnold Boldt approaches the high jump bar on his way to winning a gold medal at the 1976 International Olympiad for the Physically Disabled.

In addition to his success in the high jump, Arnold Boldt also held several world records and won numerous gold medals in the long jump.

track-and-field day for the students. Arnold gamely participated and soon discovered that he had great ability in the standing long jump and high jump. His impressive performances led to invitations to regional athletic meets against non-disabled students, where Boldt often won.

Arnold focused most of his efforts on the high jump. He trained on his own without any coaching or formalized team. On his farm, he built high jumps with two-by-fours and landed into a sand pit or bales of hay. During the winter months, he practised indoors by jumping over card-board boxes onto a sofa, which he eventually destroyed from the constant landings. During his teenage years, Boldt created his own unique style for the high jump. The most common jump styles used by able-bodied athletes were the straddle and Fosbury flop. Both styles used the velocity from the jumper's take-off run and the additional momentum gained from the kick-off motion of the second leg. Boldt's technique was designed to attain most of the lift from transference of the body from a vertical to horizontal position. Unlike typical high jumpers who approached the bar at a 45 degree angle, Boldt reached the take-off point almost directly in front of the crosspiece. His approach was also shorter; he took five to seven hops versus the average 10 strides for most able-bodied jumpers. So his take-off time was quicker and the motion was more compact. Boldt could not take advantage of the additional momentum from the second leg, so he created it by adding a strong double-arm swing motion to his jump. Boldt then lunged forward in a motion similar to a dive and rolled onto his back by the time he landed.

Arnold found out about the world of disabled sport through his friend Stan Holcomb. He was selected to participate in the first Paralympic Games (then called the International Olympiad for the Physically Disabled) that were held in Toronto in 1976. It would be the first formal international competition for disabled athletes — finally Boldt would compete against other athletes on equal footing. He was the main spiker for the volleyball team and was the Canadian team's best chance for medals in both the long and high jump competitions. Though the volleyball team finished fourth, Arnold fared better in the jumping competitions. He proved his ability early by taking the gold medal in the standing long jump and setting a world record of 2.96 metres.

He promised to do the same when he was scheduled to participate in the high jump three days later. There was such a buzz surrounding the event that all other events were postponed so that all athletes, coaches and spectators could watch the competition. Boldt decided to try altering his technique to the Fosbury flop, since it was the method most used by able-bodied jumpers. After a couple of failed attempts, Boldt returned to his dive-like style. He was astounded to discover that over half of the other athletes were using a similar jumping style. But Arnold beat all other competitors by over 20 centimetres with his world record jump of 1.86 metres. As a comparison, the top able-bodied female jumper in Canada at the time, Julie White, had a personal best of 1.87 metres.

For his extraordinary achievements, Boldt was voted best athlete of the Olympiad.

The next year, he began attending the University of Saskatchewan and joined the school's track team as a high jumper. Coach Lyle Sanderson helped Arnold further refine his technique to gain extra elevation on his jumps. By the time of the 1980 Paralympic Games, Boldt was reaching heights of nearly two metres. He also consistently placed in the top five of able-bodied jumpers at the collegiate level in Canada. Then just two weeks before the 1980 Olympiad in the Netherlands, Arnold fell down a stairway while carrying boxes and sprained his ankle. He still went to the Games, and even with reduced flexibility in his wrapped leg, he still managed to clear 1.96 metres in the high jump, setting a world record and winning a gold medal in both the high and long jump. The next year Boldt went to the World Championships in Rome, where he again set records in high jump.

Boldt's achievements at these games drew the attention of some note-worthy fans. Along with other top athletes, Boldt was invited to perform the high jump in a sports demonstration for Pope John Paul II and 80,000 spectators at the Olympic Stadium in Rome. Boldt also competed in the 1984 International Olympiad where he did not disappoint. He won gold again in the high jump. In 1988, the International Olympiad for the Physically Disabled was formally linked to the Olympics. Its name was changed to the Paralympic Games and the athletes would now compete in the same venue as the able-bodied athletes. Boldt went on to win gold again in the high jump at the 1988 and 1992 Games, where he was selected as the flag bearer for the Canadian Paralympic team. From 1976 to 1992, Arnold Boldt put together one of the longest winning streaks in sports history. In every international disabled athletics competition in which he competed, he won gold.

Boldt completed numerous degrees in theology and religion and received a master's degree in adult education that he puts to use today in his position as the dean of technology programs at the Saskatchewan Institute of Applied Sciences. He has been married for over 20 years and has two teenage sons. Since his retirement in 1994, sports are now more of a leisure activity for Boldt. Today, his only competition comes

After Arnold won a gold medal in the long jump at the 1976 Games, all other events were postponed so that spectators could watch him compete in the high jump.

from his sons on the mountain bike courses. For his incredible achievements at both the able-bodied and disabled levels, Arnold Boldt was inducted into the Saskatchewan Hall of Fame and the Canadian Sports Hall of Fame.

Arnold Boldt's aim was simply to push himself to jump higher. In a career that spanned nearly 20 years, Arnold Boldt's ability to soar through the air won him countless victories in parathletic competitions, including five gold medals in the high jump. His passion, talent and success at this event allowed him to completely dominate the sport and set world records. In achieving this, he helped legitimize international competition for disabled athletes.

"HIS TRAINING METHODS WERE
WAY AHEAD OF HIS TIME."

BILL McNULTY, SPORTS HISTORIAN,
ON PERCY WILLIAMS' COACH BOB GRANGER

PERCY
WILLIAMS

Trained to be the World's Fastest Man

"[Williams] credited Bob Granger with his every success."

JOHN MYER, SPORTSWRITER

WHEN COACH BOB GRANGER discovered him, Percy Williams was a scrawny 110-pound, five-foot six-inch high school student who was competing for the Vancouver sprint title — not a likely candidate to become a national hero. Two years later, Percy Williams would shock the world at the 1928 Summer Olympic Games in Amsterdam by winning the 100-metre sprint and the title of World's Fastest Man. Two days later, he accomplished a feat that no Olympic athlete has matched since; he also won the 200-metre sprint for his second gold medal of the Games.

Percy Williams was born on May 19, 1908, in Vancouver, British Columbia. When his parents divorced when he was only 10 years old, the young Percy became shy and reclusive. He went to live with his mother and would stay with her until she died in 1978. At age 15, the already small and frail Percy was diagnosed with rheumatic fever. Doctors advised him not to engage in any competitive physical activities, since too much strain on his heart could be dangerous. But the determined Percy ignored their instructions. He felt that the pressure from his athletic peers to compete was more important than his health. "You were a bum if you didn't compete," he later said regarding his decision to ignore his doctors' orders and continue competing in track.

Percy Williams bounds from the starting blocks in an athletics event at the Summer Games in Amsterdam. He was known as the World's Fastest Man in 1928.

Despite his stature and health issues, Percy was a natural runner. He did not love running, but he had innate talent; he ran because he was good at it. In the summer of 1926, high school athlete Percy Williams ran to a draw with Vancouver sprint champion Wally Scott. Scott's coach, Bob Granger, was impressed by Williams' performance; he saw the potential of an Olympic winner. Granger approached Williams soon after the race and told him, "I can make you a champion."

Percy trusted the lively Scotsman and soon began a novel training regime. Most coaches of the day measured a runner's success based on a stopwatch. Bob Granger, a janitor and part-time coach, was convinced that a sprinter had to be trained to beat his competition, not a clock. He focused on developing Percy's instincts to react to situations. He would place another runner 4.5 to 13.5 metres ahead of Percy at the beginning of a 100-metre sprint. This technique taught Williams to accelerate throughout the race. Granger also focused on helping Williams develop an explosive start. He placed a mattress against a wall and would have Williams set into his starting crouch a few paces away. Again and again, Percy would explode from his starting crouch into the mattress.

Granger also understood Williams' delicate condition, so he insisted on rest, comfort and warmth for the young runner. While other competitors were warming up by running around the track, Granger wrapped Williams in a thermal blanket and had him conserve his energy by lying down. In cold weather, he rubbed Williams with coconut oil and dressed him in numerous layers to conserve body heat. He also made sure that Williams only raced sparingly — in his entire running career, he ran in fewer than 100 competitions. Under Granger's watchful eye, Williams' form, time and results improved steadily, so much so that the innovative coach soon dropped all other runners to focus solely on Percy.

In the 1920s winning races in the Vancouver area was one thing, but to get national attention Williams needed to make his mark in the East, particularly in the Hamilton-Toronto area, which was the unofficial capital of Canadian track-and-field at the time. As the top sprinter in British Columbia, Percy went to the 1927 Canadian Championships in Hamilton. At the time, track-and-field officials did not consider coaches to be important to an athlete's success, so Granger had to make his own

Though he was denied a position on the 1927 Canadian Championship team, Percy Williams won the National Championships and two Olympic gold medals the following year.

arrangements to get to the Canadian Championships. He worked his way across the country as a dishwasher and server on the Canadian Pacific Railways. Unfortunately, however, after all their efforts to get there, Granger and Williams were the victims of poor planning by the event organizers. Williams was one of six runners to qualify for the 100-metre final, but there were only five lanes on the track. The organizers tossed a coin to decide which finalist would not run and Percy lost. He would have to wait a year to avenge this ill fate. He did return for the 1928 Canadian Championships, and he surprised the spectators by winning not only the 100 metres, but the 200-metre final as well. He also won a place on Canada's 1928 Summer Olympics team.

Granger was convinced that Percy needed his help in order to win at the 1928 Amsterdam Summer Olympic Games, so he applied to the Canadian Olympic Committee to travel with Percy as his coach. The committee rejected his application; it had already chosen Captain Cornelius, a local high school coach from Hamilton, to train the Canadian track team. But Granger was determined to be at those Games, so he made his way to Amsterdam as a deck hand on a cattle boat. During his voyage he transmitted training techniques to Williams by radio.

Percy's discipline and performance deteriorated without Granger, but when the runner and coach reunited in Amsterdam, Percy's training got back on track quickly. The two worked at the track by day and on his starts at night in the hotel. Athletes in adjoining rooms could hear a chorus of "run, run, thump" as Percy burst into the mattress that Granger placed against the wall.

Williams' first race was the 100-metre sprint. To select the six athletes who would compete in the final, the sprinters had to run a series of heats. The top two runners in each race proceeded to the next heat, while the losers bowed out of the competition. Williams won his first three heats and placed second in the semi-finals. This earned him a spot in the final. When the runners lined up for the final on July 30, 1928, Williams was the last runner to take his mark because Granger had wrapped him in a thermal blanket to keep him warm. The race began with two false starts, but Williams kept his composure. When the starter's pistol went off for a third time, Williams broke into the lead and never looked back, winning his first gold medal and the title of World's Fastest Man.

The 200-metre final was only two days away, and Olympic officials worried that the 100-metre event might have drained Williams. They questioned whether he had the necessary focus to continue competing at the Olympic level. They offered to let Williams withdraw from the race, but he refused. Instead, he won his first two heats and the 200-metre final to win his second gold medal.

Few athletes have mastered both the 100-metre and 200-metre events. Though both are sprints, the two are different races that require different skills. The 100-metre is a race straight down the track, but the 200-metre is a half lap of the track; it demands that the runner also be skilled at

*Percy Williams' unique training methods designed by his coach, Bob Granger,
were key to his running success.*

Percy Williams of Vancouver crosses the finish line to win the gold medal in the 100-metre race at the 1928 Amsterdam Olympics.

accelerating through the corners. Percy Williams showed the world that he had both speed and skill. He took on a field of 84 of the fastest men in the world and beat them all in these two very different races.

Williams returned home to Canada as a hero. Knowing that Percy Williams would receive many scholarship offers from top American universities, city officials in Vancouver proposed that he attend the University of British Columbia and to pay him a $25,000 scholarship. The city never paid the full amount and Williams dropped out after one year. Meanwhile, Bob Granger was offered numerous coaching positions at top U.S. universities, including Harvard and Yale. He turned them down so he could continue coaching Percy Williams.

After the Olympic Games, Williams was invited to a series of 21 track competitions over 22 days in nine different U.S. cities. Sports historian Bill McNulty refers to this track series as the "Iron Guts" tour, because Williams ran unfamiliar distances and on surfaces that he had never experienced before. He had to contend with the effects of travelling to nine different cities in such a short time period, while his competition did not. Yet Percy Williams managed to finish first in 19 races and second in the other two. He also set a world record in the 100-metre in August 1930. He was given another chance to defend his Olympic titles by competing in the 1932 Olympics in Los Angeles. Unfortunately, however, Percy couldn't repeat his legendary performance. He had suffered a leg injury at the 1931 British Empire Games. Williams did not even make it to the finals. When the Olympics ended, Williams never raced again.

When he came back to Canada, Williams went to business school and became an insurance agent. He never married and remained highly reclusive. He later suffered two strokes and endured agonizing arthritis in all of his joints. In 1982, Percy Williams committed suicide to end his suffering.

Bob Granger never found another athlete like Percy Williams. He too lived a lonely life, moving from one job to another. He also passed away alone, 12 years before his protégé, in 1970.

Percy Williams established an incredible running legacy. With the aid of the innovative and dedicated Bob Granger, the small, fragile athlete became the world's fastest man in 1928 and was virtually unbeatable over the next two years. In 1950, the Canadian Press named him the greatest track athlete of the first half century. In 1972, they named him Canada's all-time greatest Olympic athlete. He was also elected to the British Columbia and Canadian Sports Halls of Fame. Bob Granger never received similar honours. But he should be credited for unlocking Percy Williams' potential and then building him into one of the greatest track athletes in sports history.

Chapter Six

DETERMINATION

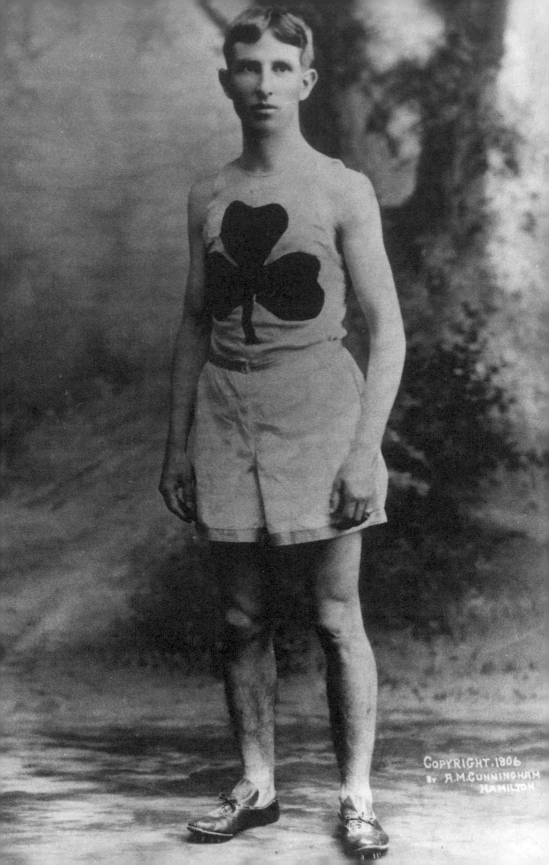

COPYRIGHT. 1906
BY A.M.CUNNINGHAM
HAMILTON

WILLIAM (BILL)
SHERRING

Long Shot

"[Running] seemed more natural to me than walking."

BILL SHERRING

BILL SHERRING FELT confident that he could win the 1906 Olympic marathon; his bigger problem was figuring out how he was going to get to the Olympic Games in Athens. He had little savings of his own and his sports club and the government were unable to send him there to compete. Instead, a local bartender, who was a fan of the long-distance runner, gave Sherring some money and a tip on a horse that he expected to win. The horse came in and Sherring took his winnings to buy his ticket to Greece. In a few months, he would shock the world by winning the gold medal. His newfound celebrity status afforded him the luxury of never having to worry about money again.

Born on September 10, 1877, in Hamilton, Ontario, William J. "Bill" Sherring was a natural runner. He was said to have run perpetually as a child and throughout his youth. By age 16, he was winning races of various distances at fairs throughout Ontario. Hamilton held one of the best known long-distance races during the late 1800s and early 1900s called the "Round the Bay" race. The course of about 30 kilometres curved around Burlington Bay. During these races, Bill Sherring established himself as one of the best long-distance runners in Canada. He came third in 1897 and won the race in 1899 and 1903. Sherring also competed

Olympic marathoner Bill Sherring wears his St. Patrick's Athletics Club uniform.

in the U.S. whenever possible. In 1900, he ran in the Boston Marathon. At the 21-mile mark, Sherring collapsed at the side of the road, but he managed to get up and walk until his shakiness settled. Then he began passing runners all the way to the finish line and captured second place. But even with his North American success, Bill Sherring was virtually unknown in Europe.

When Olympic organizers announced that they were going to hold the Panhellenic Olympic Games in 1906 between the typical four-year interval that separated the 1904 St. Louis and 1908 London Olympic Games, Sherring knew that he wanted to compete. But he had a problem. Sherring worked as a brakeman with Grand Trunk Railway. He earned enough to support his modest lifestyle, but he did not have nearly enough money to pay for a trip to Greece. At the time there was no Canadian Olympic Association, and the various levels of government did not provide financial assistance to athletes. His own sports club, the St. Patrick's Athletic Club, claimed to have no money available, although in the end it did provide $75 to help pay for the voyage. Sherring luckily had a fan who worked as a bartender at the Commercial Hotel. The bartender believed in Bill and gave him $50 to support Sherring's dream. He also gave Sherring a tip that the hotel owner's horse, Cicely, who was racing at Woodbine Racetrack, was likely to win and pay well at high odds. Since $50 would not be nearly enough to pay for the trip, Bill bet on the horse and won. With his winnings, a donation from the St. Patrick's Athletic Club and his own life savings, Bill Sherring bought a third-class ticket on a ship set to arrive in Athens, Greece, at the end of February 1906.

When Sherring arrived in Greece for the Panhellenic Olympic Games, he had to train and support himself. Sherring took odd jobs running tours in English for American and British visitors and served as a porter at the train station. He also ran as often as he could, completing the marathon course 10 times before the official race. Sherring's lack of funds and heavy work and training schedule took their toll on the five-foot seven-inch runner. Between the time of his departure from Hamilton and the start of the marathon, Sherring lost over 20 pounds. Yet he was still

Bill Sherring became one of Canada's earliest Olympic heroes after winning the marathon at the 1906 Olympic Games in Athens, Greece.

confident of victory. He wrote to his brother Jack less than two weeks before the race to tell him, "I think that I will win, for I feel strong and good."

On May 1, Athens was abuzz for the big race, the final event of the 1906 Olympic Games. All stores were closed and over 150,000 spectators lined the course and filled the stadium where the race was to end. The 26-mile-and-385-yard steep course retraced the original route travelled by the Greek messenger who carried the news to Athens of the Greek victory at the Battle of Marathon in 490 BC — the same route of the first marathon of the modern Games.

At 3:00 p.m., 67 runners lined up for the start of the race. Sherring relied on his own judgment and stamina for his racing strategy. He held back, letting some runners pass, knowing that they would not have the strength to continue at their quick pace. By the 12th mile, he had already caught most of the tired runners and was soon running with the leader, William Frank of Great Britain. At just past 18 miles, Sherring decided to pass Frank. Knowing that he did not have enough energy to challenge, Frank is reported to have yelled out, "Well, good bye Billy." Sherring then built such a lead over the other runners that he was able to walk part of the last eight miles to conserve his energy. When he finally arrived at the Olympic stadium, seven minutes ahead of his nearest competitor, Crown Prince Constantine of Greece was so excited that he went down to the track and ran most of the last lap with the Canadian champion. In the horrible 98 degree heat of the day, Sherring lost 14 pounds. He crossed the finish line at 2:51:23.6.

For winning the coveted race, Sherring was presented with symbols of Greek folklore: a huge marble statue of Minerva, a bust of Hermes and a goat, along with his gold medal. When he returned to Hamilton, a torch-light procession was held in his honour and he received over $5,000 from the federal, provincial and municipal governments. Sherring was also given the post of chief clerk at the parcel post department of Canadian Customs. He held this post until his retirement at age 65. Sherring married and had five children. He passed away on September 6, 1964.

The Olympics was Sherring's last race as an amateur. He turned professional shortly after returning to Hamilton to capitalize on his newfound celebrity status. His hometown of Hamilton, Ontario, also benefited from his victory — the city developed a marathon tradition with the "Round the Bay" run. It honoured the star runner by naming races and a school after him. Sherring also became one of the first athletes elected to the Canadian Sports Hall of Fame.

Bill Sherring's endurance, courage and belief in his abilities made him one of Canada's first Olympic heroes. His gold medal run in Athens, Greece, in 1906 was legendary, but he would never have made it there if not for the generosity of a bartender and the sure-footedness of a horse.

GEORGE
HUNGERFORD &
ROGER JACKSON

Unlikely Heroes

"It seemed so unfair, I was about to achieve my dream … and it was all being taken away."

GEORGE HUNGERFORD ON DEVELOPING MONONUCLEOSIS
LESS THAN THREE MONTHS BEFORE THE 1964 OLYMPIC GAMES

THREE MONTHS BEFORE the 1964 Summer Olympic Games in Tokyo, Japan, one illness put two Olympic dreams at risk. George Hungerford was a key member of the eight-member rowing crew who were on their way to compete in Tokyo. But George came down with mononucleosis and was pulled from the team. When alternate Wayne Pretty was selected to replace Hungerford on the eight-member team, Roger Jackson lost his coxless partner and almost lost his chance to compete. When Hungerford returned five weeks later eager to begin training for the Games, he was not Jackson's ideal replacement partner. Hungerford was still trying to recover his strength and would sleep between practices to recuperate. But within weeks the two began to work like a team that had been training together for years. In Tokyo they posted the fastest time in the qualifying heats and then achieved the unthinkable, a gold medal — the only one that Canada would win at those Olympic Games.

Born on January 2, 1944, in Vancouver, George Hungerford was a natural athlete. He began rowing in the 11th grade, but was more interested in other school sports, including basketball, squash and his passion, rugby. But the full-contact sport of rugby was hard on his body; he suffered a recurring shoulder injury that prevented him from playing.

Roger Jackson (front) and George Hungerford celebrate their unexpected gold medal win in the coxless pairs rowing event at the 1964 Tokyo Olympics.

When he had to have his arm surgically pinned, Hungerford was prompted to look for another sport. When he graduated from high school, George went on to study at the University of British Columbia, a school that boasted the top rowing team in the country. The powerful six-foot four-inch George Hungerford tried out for the team, hoping that the tough work-outs would get him back into top shape after his layoff from the shoulder surgery. By early spring 1964, George Hungerford was on the varsity squad, rowing on the four-person and eight-person teams. At the end of the school year, George set out to join the eight-person crew of the Vancouver Rowing Club. There was no national rowing team at the time, so each of the top clubs in Canada competed against each other to win the right to represent Canada at the Olympics. Hungerford felt confident that if he could make the Vancouver team, he would be going to Tokyo in less than six months to compete in the Olympics.

Roger Jackson moved to Vancouver in the spring of 1964 for the same reason: to make the rowing team and then compete at the Olympic Games in Tokyo. Born on January 14, 1942, in Toronto, Jackson did not take up rowing until university. In high school, he was a good athlete in football, basketball and hockey, but he was not a standout. When he arrived at the University of Western Ontario in London, Ontario, he decided that he wanted to try something new, so he took up rowing. The six-foot five-inch athlete took to the sport immediately. He rowed each year with the team and then each summer with the London Rowing Club. Jackson went on to pursue a master's degree at the University of Toronto, where he continued to row as a member of the Toronto Argonauts rowing team. He knew that the Argonaut Rowing Club was putting a team together to challenge for the right to represent Canada at the Olympics, but he also knew that the top rowing club in Canada was in Vancouver. Feeling confident, he travelled to Vancouver at the end of the school year with hopes of making the club.

One of the reasons the Vancouver club was so well regarded was its heavy training schedule. While most clubs practised once a day, the Vancouver club was on the water twice each day for 12 practices a week. Both Hungerford and Jackson demonstrated extraordinary ability, deter-mination and devotion to the sport. They both secured spots on the

Vancouver boats. Hungerford was selected for the eights and Jackson for the four-member crews.

Unfortunately, just a few days before the regatta where Canada's Olympic teams would be selected, one of the members of the fours crew was injured. The team's replacement did not have the same control of the boat or power in his stroke and Jackson's crew lost its race. Hungerford's squad had better luck, winning its race and a berth at the Olympic Games. Team organizers decided, however, that the Vancouver squad should select two alternates for the eight-member crew. The alternates would also train and compete as a coxless pair (two-person team without a coxswain, who steers the boat and dictates the stroke rate). Roger Jackson and Wayne Pretty were chosen as the alternates and thereby given a chance to compete at the Olympics.

Shortly after he returned to Vancouver, George Hungerford became incredibly fatigued and more drained than usual at training sessions. When he discovered that he had the respiratory virus mononucleosis, he was devastated. The virus, which causes fatigue, fever, headaches, sore muscles, swelling of the lymph glands and enlargement of the spleen, has only one cure — rest. Hungerford knew that to conquer the illness, he would have to stay in bed and forfeit his place on the eight-member team. One of the alternates, Wayne Pretty, was chosen to take George's place on the eights. This left Roger Jackson without a pairs partner.

But neither Hungerford nor Jackson gave up. Roger Jackson still practised every day and trained as hard as anyone else on the team. George Hungerford did everything to battle his illness and get back to training as soon as possible. Five weeks later, when a doctor told Hungerford that his symptoms had disappeared, George was elated. Though he wasn't fully recovered, he began training immediately. By doing so, he put his body at risk — his still-enlarged spleen could potentially rupture and there was also a possibility that he could relapse. Wayne Pretty kept his spot on the eights, while Hungerford became Jackson's new partner for the coxless pairs. Jackson was happy to have a pairs partner again, but was wary of Hungerford's ability. George still wasn't back to full strength and had never raced in a pairs competition before. Jackson decided that the only way to put his team in the lead would be to push himself and his partner.

George Hungerford (left) and teammate Roger Jackson (right) receive the gold medal for their victory in the coxless pairs rowing at the 1964 Olympic Summer Games.

In pairs rowing, each athlete strokes one oar on opposite sides of the shell, an exercise that requires perfect coordination between the two rowers. Any movement out of unison can cause the shell to veer in one direction, reducing its speed and forcing the rowers to compensate to get the boat back in line, further slowing down the shell. On paper Hungerford and Jackson seemed a perfect pair; they were almost the same height, weight and reach. But when the two began training, Hungerford could not keep pace with Jackson's powerful and frequent strokes and the shell would be going in circles. Hungerford also had problems steering the shell. As the bowman at the back of the boat, George had a metal cord next to his foot, which controls the movement of the rudder and the direction of the boat. They decided to simply remove the rudder, which forced the rowers to be in perfect synchronization. It also helped cut seconds from their time caused by eliminating the drag of the rudder on the water.

With each day, Hungerford gained more strength and the two worked more and more as a team. Hungerford still needed to nap between training sessions to restore his energy, but he was no longer getting pulled in circles by Jackson and he was starting to keep pace. When the teams arrived in Tokyo for the Olympic Games, the Canadians received a much-needed gift from the Americans. To replace Hungerford and Jackson's old and inferior pairs shell, the University of Washington team lent them a shell that had been used in previous competitions.

Jackson and Hungerford were tested early. Their qualifying heat was scheduled for the first day of the Olympic competition, October 11, 1964. During the race, the Canadian pair had to not only outpace the other teams, but they also had to steer clear of a Finnish crew that was veering into their lane. Even with this challenge, Hungerford and Jackson posted the fastest qualifying time of all teams, a feat which allowed them to move directly to the finals instead of having to compete in a semi-final race. Hungerford was able to spend the two days between the races resting and conserving his strength.

On race day Hungerford and Jackson, not expected to challenge for a medal, were placed in the outside lane for the coxless pairs final. There was a false start on the first attempt, which benefited the Canadians, who hadn't had a clean start. On the second start, Hungerford and Jackson were in perfect unison. The team knew that they would have to pull ahead and build a lead over the others by the midpoint of the race because Hungerford would not have the energy to give a strong kick to the finish. They raced exactly according to plan. By the 800- to 900-metre mark of the 2,000-metre race, they pulled into the lead and increased that lead to a boat length and a half over the next 400 metres. During the final 500-metre stretch, Jackson slowed down his stroke rate instead of sprinting for the finish, fearful that he would pull the boat out of line if Hungerford could not keep up. But with about 100 metres left, Jackson saw the Netherlands catching up through a strong sprint and he called on George to increase his stroke rate. Out of sheer adrenalin and fierce will power, George managed to do it and the pair held off the Dutch team to capture the gold. Their victory was such a surprise that not a single Canadian media group was there to interview or photograph the winning Canadian team. The Vancouver eight-man crew unfortunately did not fare as well; they lost their qualifying heat and finished ninth.

When Hungerford and Jackson returned to Canada, they competed together only a few more times. George Hungerford retired from the sport after he and Jackson lost at the Henley regatta in the U.K., in 1965. He went to law school, married and had four children. Roger Jackson completed his master's degree and his PhD, but continued to row, representing Canada at the 1968 and 1972 Olympic Games. He married, had three children, and became a professor of kinesiology and director of the Sports Medicine Centre at the University of Calgary.

For their achievements, George Hungerford and Roger Jackson were also awarded the Lou Marsh trophy in 1964 and were inducted to the Canadian Sports Hall of Fame that same year. The two later became Officers of the Order of Canada.

Both George Hungerford and Dr. Roger Jackson remain involved in Canadian sports. Hungerford was a founding director of the Olympic Club and was on the successful Vancouver 2010 Winter Olympics bid committee. Jackson was a member of the Pan-American Sports Organization's executive committee for 17 years; was elected president of the Canadian Olympic Association for three terms in the 1980s; and was one of the four original members of the successful Calgary 1988 Winter Olympics bid committee.

Hungerford and Jackson proved that mental discipline in sports can be as important as skill and physical ability. Their victory remains a symbol of what teamwork, commitment and mental resolve can accomplish.

Dr. Roger Jackson (left) receives the Volunteer of the Year Award in 1988 from Allen Rae, President of the Sports Federation of Canada.

DONALD KING MEMORIAL TROPHY
DONATED BY
THE CANADIAN CRICKET ASSOCIATION
IN MEMORY OF
DONALD KING, C.M., M.B.E. 1906-1977
TO THE
SPORTS FEDERATION OF CANADA
TO BE AWARDED
OUTSTANDING SERVICE AS A VOLUNTEER
IN SPORT ADMINISTRATION

Chapter Seven

GRACE
IN DEFEAT

SYLVIE, FRÉCHETTE

Tragedy, Injustice, Victory

"I had one way left to protest: to swim better than I had ever swum before ... to show the world who the real champion was."

SYLVIE FRÉCHETTE, *GOLD AT LAST*

NINETEEN-NINETY-TWO was supposed to be Sylvie Fréchette's year. After 18 years of training and competition in synchronized swimming, she was going to the Olympics as a favourite to win the gold medal. She was also engaged to be married the following summer and was soon to embark on a career as a spokesperson for the National Bank of Canada. But Sylvie's world would suddenly come crashing down on her, testing her resolve and mental stamina. Shortly before she was to compete for Olympic gold, tragedy struck — her grandfather passed away and later her fiancé committed suicide. Then she was the ill-fated recipient of a technical judging error during her Olympic performance. But Sylvie demonstrated a remarkable grace and determination. She managed to compete at her best under these trying circumstances — a feat that made her a hero and ultimately an Olympic gold medal winner.

Sylvie was born on June 27, 1967, in Montreal, Quebec. Unfortunately, at an early age she faced the first of many tragedies in her life. Her father René, a bus driver, was killed in a crash when she was only four years old. Sylvie, her brother, Martin, and her mother had to move in with her grandparents to make ends meet. Not long after, her grandfather assumed the role of surrogate father and became Sylvie's first swimming coach.

Sylvie Fréchette dazzles the crowd at the 1996 Atlanta Games on her way to capturing a silver medal in the synchronized swimming team event.

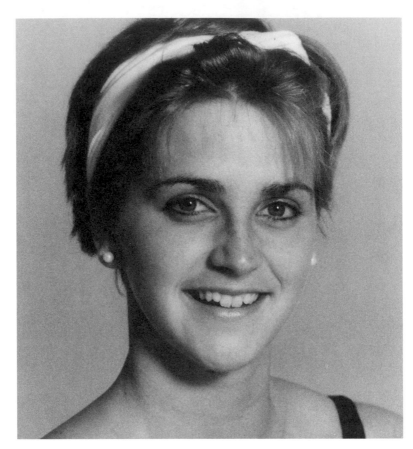

In her efforts both in and out of the pool, Sylvie Fréchette has made a significant contribution to the world of Canadian Sport. Her determination and grace continue to inspire Canadians.

At the age of seven, Sylvie was already an avid swimmer. At the pool, she noticed some girls practising synchronized swimming. She was awestruck. How did they manage to keep their arms out of the water without sinking? Sylvie decided she wanted to join these girls in their training and in their performances, so she signed up.

Soon it was hard to get Sylvie to concentrate on anything other than being in the pool. At age 11, she took part in her first synchronized swimming duet competition. Her team came 23rd out of 24 entrants. Sylvie knew she could do better. For the next two years she dedicated herself to training — she worked hard, and steadily improved. At the Canadian Junior Championships, her discipline paid off — she won both the solo and the duet events. Shortly thereafter, Sylvie graduated from the juniors to become one of the eight members of the Canadian national synchronized swimming team in 1983.

At the same time Sylvie was establishing herself as a synchronized swimmer, the sport itself experienced its own growth. At the 1984 Summer Olympic Games in Los Angeles, synchronized swimming was included as a medal sport for the first time. Sylvie continued to rise in the ranks, but she was overshadowed by another swimmer, Carolyn Waldo, the number one soloist in Canada. Waldo competed and won a silver medal at the Games in L.A. Sylvie continued to train and develop her skills. She worked on increasing her natural flexibility and strength; both would enable her to make cleaner and stronger movements than most other competitors. (She was more flexible because she had an extraordinary ability to dislocate all of her joints.)

By 1988, Sylvie was the number two-ranked synchronized swimmer in Canada. Many people thought she would compete at the Seoul Olympics in the duet event. Unfortunately, however, Carolyn Waldo, still the number one-ranked synchronized swimmer, was already paired with the third-ranked Michelle Cameron. After some deliberation, Synchro Canada officials decided that this team should remain intact — Sylvie would have to wait until 1992 for a chance to win an Olympic medal.

Carolyn Waldo won double gold at the 1988 Games — as a soloist and as a member of the duet. But later that year, Waldo retired from the sport, leaving Sylvie the number one-ranked swimmer in Canada. She would finally have her chance. At the 1989 World Cup, Fréchette won silver as a soloist, silver for the team event and bronze in the duet. But at the same event in 1991, she was not to be denied. Of the total of 14 marks presented for the long program, Fréchette scored seven perfect 10s, setting a new world record and winning a gold medal. She instantly became the favourite for Olympic gold in Barcelona. In September, Sylvie got engaged to boyfriend and roommate Sylvain Lake. The couple decided to delay their wedding until after the next Olympics in 1992 so that Sylvie could focus on training for the Games.

Unfortunately, only months after the engagement, Sylvie's grandfather passed away. His death was hard on Sylvie — it felt as if she had lost a father for the second time. Then, just days before she was scheduled to leave for Barcelona, tragedy struck again. On July 18, 1992, Sylvie arrived at her home and could smell gas in the air. She found her fiancé, Sylvain, dead from the inhalation of car exhaust fumes. He had committed suicide, leaving no note or explanation for Sylvie of why he had taken his own life. She was devastated and seriously contemplated cancelling her ticket to Barcelona and abandoning her lifelong dream of going to the Olympics. But with remarkable clarity at a time of such overwhelming tragedy, Sylvie recognized that the only thing that could save her from serious depression was swimming.

When she arrived in Barcelona, Sylvie's main task was to get her focus back on the competition. In her quest for an Olympic gold medal, she had trained and made sacrifices for 18 years. She knew she was within reach, but would have to find inner strength and persevere to make her dream come true.

The solo event in synchronized swimming is divided into two competitions: the compulsory figures and the long program. The figures in particular require extreme concentration because the judges look for the most minor of flaws to separate the winners from the pack; an extra space left between the legs or a movement that is not quite fully extended can cost a swimmer her chance at a medal. Despite the tragedies in her personal life, Fréchette managed to perform all her movements flawlessly. But after her performance, there seemed to be some commotion among the judges, and there was an unusually long delay before the marks were posted. When her results were finally put up on the board, the marks ranged from 9.2 to 9.7, with the exception of one extremely low score of 8.7. The Brazilian judge, Ana Maria da Silveira Lobo, had inadvertently pushed the wrong button. When da Silveira realized her error, she implored the assistant referee from Japan to change her mark to 9.7. "I wanted a 9.7, not 8.7," she pleaded. As the Brazilian judge cried on the sidelines, the Canadian team launched a formal appeal. It was rejected by the head judge and the appeals judge. The error gave the American swimmer, Kristen Babb-Sprague, an insurmountable lead and put Fréchette in fourth place going into the long program.

Sylvie Fréchette celebrates the silver medal she won in the synchronized swimming event at the 1992 Olympics Games in Barcelona. Due to a judging mistake at the Games, Sylvie was later awarded the gold medal.

Sylvie had less than a day to come to terms with her newest misfortune. Though she knew she could not win a gold medal, she was determined to prove to the world, technical error or not, that she was the synchronized swimming world champion. She swam her long program with all of her heart and gave the performance of her life. Her three-and-a-half-minute routine was the most difficult of all those performed that day. She tested her superior arm strength with a host of complex out-of-water leg movements which required her to spend nearly two-thirds of her routine upside down and underwater. Sylvie also tested her lung capacity. During one portion of her routine, she spent an astonishing 42 seconds without a breath. But she had accomplished her goal — Sylvie received the highest marks of all competitors for the long program. Had she received the 9.7 that she deserved, her combined scores would have earned her the gold. But with the officially recorded 8.7, it was not enough. Kristen Babb-Sprague won the gold, Sylvie Fréchette the silver. Sylvie made no protests, graciously accepted her silver medal, and stood proudly beside Babb-Sprague on the podium.

International Olympic Committee Vice-President Dick Pound of Montreal was not so gracious. He continued to petition on Fréchette's behalf. He presented his case to the international swimming body, FINA (La Fédération Internationale de Natation) and spoke to the International Olympic Committee's president, Juan Antonio Samaranch. His argument was ultimately persuasive. Sixteen months later, in front of thousands of cheering Montreal fans, the IOC presented Sylvie Fréchette the gold medal she deserved.

Sylvie retired briefly from swimming, only to return to the sport for the next Olympic Games in Atlanta, where she won a silver medal in the team event. She also completed her bachelor of physical education degree at the Université de Montreal; worked as a sports analyst for Radio-Canada; hosted her own TV show, *Simplément Sylvie* (*Simply Sylvie*), and wrote her best-selling autobiography, *Gold at Last*. She also worked with the National Bank of Canada to found a bursary program that provides $75,000 in annual support to upcoming amateur Canadian athletes. Sylvie currently works as assistant artistic coordinator and aquatic designer for Cirque du Soleil's "O" show. She married in the summer of 2000 and is the doting mother of a little girl, Emma.

Sylvie Fréchette returned from a brief retirement to help the synchronized swimming team capture a silver medal at the Olympic Games in Atlanta.

Fréchette's many sports achievements led to her induction into the Canadian Sports Hall of Fame in 1999. She was also voted Quebec athlete of the year in both 1992 and 1993 and awarded the Ordère Olympique du Canada in 1994. Sylvie Fréchette was a true champion — her steadfast focus, her ability to compete at her best despite the tragedies that both preceded and surrounded the 1992 Barcelona Olympics and the quiet dignity she displayed during and after those Games was remarkable. In recognition of this, the Canadian Sports Federation created an award in her name — an award that is now presented to athletes who overcome adversity to triumph in their sport.

JAMIE SALÉ &

DAVID PELLETIER

Golden Performance

"We won the silver but had a gold medal performance."

JAMIE SALÉ

"It's an embarrassment to the sport."

LORI NICHOL, SALÉ AND PELLETIER'S CHOREOGRAPHER

THEY SKATED a flawless long program, worthy of a gold medal. But when the results came in, Jamie Salé's tears and David Pelletier's look of exasperation told the story. In a five-to-four decision by the judges, the Canadian pair finished second to Russian skaters Elena Berezhnaya and Anton Sikharulidze. But their Olympic story did not end there. A media frenzy erupted as corruption in figure skating judging was exposed — and Jamie Salé and David Pelletier were caught in the middle. But throughout the ordeal, the skaters' tact, modesty and charm won them worldwide fans and, ultimately, their well-deserved gold medals.

Jamie Salé and David Pelletier followed two very different paths on their way to the Olympics. Jamie Salé was born on April 21, 1977, in Red Deer, Alberta. A natural skater, she put on figure skates for the first time at age five and instantly took to the sport and the spotlight. A live Kurt Browning performance and the positive buzz that surrounded the 1988 Calgary Olympics, particularly Elizabeth Manley's silver medal-winning performance, inspired Jamie Salé to become an Olympic medalist herself. In 1990, she moved to Edmonton to train with Jan Ullmark. She was a dedicated athlete with natural talent which led to quick success. At the Canadian Championships in 1992, she won a bronze medal in the novice

David Pelletier embraces Jamie Salé during their free skate performance at the 2002 Olympic Games in Salt Lake City.

pairs with partner Jason Turner. The two skaters advanced to win the Canadian Junior Pairs Championship in that same year. With their victory, the pair moved to the top amateur grouping, seniors, but ultimately split apart after poor performances in international competitions in 1994. Jamie Salé continued to skate competitively, focusing mainly on singles competition.

David Pelletier was born on November 22, 1974, in Sayabec, Quebec. Like Salé, David also took to the ice at a young age; he was only three years old. But figure skating wasn't his first love. Pelletier originally took up figure skating to help improve his hockey skills. Though he was a gifted skater, he preferred to play hockey and would often skip figure skating practices to play with his friends. But the 1988 Calgary Olympics made David finally look at figure skating seriously. He was impressed by the attention and glory the Olympic medalists earned and he longed for the same for himself. Pelletier decided that figure skating would be his key to attaining it. In order to compete at the international level, he moved from the small town of Sayabec to Rimouski to train with coach David Graham. In 1991, Pelletier and his partner at the time, Julie Laporte, won a bronze medal in the novice pairs Canadian Championships and by 1993 they were the Canadian junior pairs champions. David switched partners in 1994 to join Allison Gaynor. By 1995, the two began making headway, finishing 15th at the World Championships.

But 1996 and 1997 were frustrating periods for both skaters. Despite finishing 12th at the International Junior Championships in 1995, Salé failed to earn a place in either the 1996 or 1997 senior Canadian Championships. In 1997, Pelletier split with Allison Gaynor after a second disappointing finish at the Canadian championships. He skated one year with Caroline Roy, but after a sixth place showing at the Canadian championships, the pair went their separate ways.

David Pelletier was determined to give his Olympic dream one last shot. He pleaded with internationally acclaimed coach Richard Gauthier to take him under his wing. Gauthier agreed, but under two conditions: Pelletier had to do everything that was asked of him, and he had to skate with a new pairs partner, Jamie Salé. Gauthier arranged for a four-day tryout in Edmonton. Salé and Pelletier had already had a brief tryout in 1996, but it was unsuccessful. At the time, neither Salé nor Pelletier felt that their timing or chemistry clicked.

But both skaters were willing to try again. This time the tryout was perfect. Within days, Salé and Pelletier were nailing lifts, turns, jumps and side-by-side skating that usually takes a new skating pair up to two years to master. Jamie Salé quickly packed her bags and moved to Montreal to join David and train under Gauthier. Their chemistry and ability to work off each other — Pelletier the perfectionist and Salé the performer — brought instant results. They took two third place finishes at major international competitions in 1998: Skate Canada and the NHK in Japan. In 1999, they came second at the Canadian Championships, but were forced to withdraw from the world competition, because Pelletier had a herniated disc.

The charming pair went on to earn more and more titles and even more fans. In 1999 they won the Skate America competition with their long program skated to "Love Story." In 2000 they won their first Canadian Championship, scoring five perfect 6.0 scores, and went on to capture the same title the next two years in a row. Their success in Canada spread to the international stage. The pair came fourth at the World Championships in 2000 and then they won the competition in 2001. When they arrived at Salt Lake City, Utah, for the 2002 Olympic Games, they had established themselves as the team to beat.

Most experts in the sport felt that their strongest competition would be from the Russian pair, Elena Berezhnaya and Anton Sikharulidze. Salé and Pelletier were considered to have the edge, since they had defeated the Russian team on six of the nine occasions when they'd faced them. But this was the Olympics and in the sport of figure skating, politics is often as important as performance. Judges in figure skating have frequently been accused of vote swapping and deal making, particularly in the ice dancing competitions. Some commentators even argued that Russia's success in international competitions since 1990 was in part a result of the disproportionate share of votes that former Soviet and Eastern bloc countries held in the International Skating Union since the breakup of the Soviet Union. If the accusations were true, the Canadians would have to skate perfectly to win gold since four of the nine judges were sympathetic to the Russians.

Pairs figure skating is made up of two components: the short and long programs. For each program, the teams are judged on both the artistry of their production and the execution of certain required elements: jumps, throws and side-by-side skating. For their short program, Salé and Pelletier performed a sizzling tango to "La Jalousie." Their presentation was playful and they landed each element with the exception of their final pose, when they both fell to the ice. Since the fall did not

Jamie Salé and David Pelletier's inspiring performance at the 2002 Olympic Games ultimately led to Canada's first gold medal in figure skating since the 1960s.

occur during the required elements, judges did not have to deduct marks. The Canadians were second to the Russian pair going into the long program.

During the practice skate, minutes before the last group of skaters would complete their long programs, Jamie Salé collided with the Russian skater, Anton Sikharulidze. She was knocked to the ice. For a few moments, Salé could not move. When she got to her feet, she felt

Jamie Sale and David Pelletier react as their marks are posted for their pairs free skate at the Winter Games in Salt Lake City, Utah.

pain in her head and stomach and numbness in her arm. Salé left the ice and waited for the Russian pair to skate.

Sikharulidze and Berezhnaya had some unsteady throws and Sikharuldize stepped out of a technical double axel combination. Although they received high marks, 5.7s and 5.8s for technique and mainly 5.9s for presentation, the Canadians had an opening. Salé put the pain from her fall aside and with Pelletier responded by skating the performance of her career. Choreographed to the famous "Love Story," the pair's performance was extraordinary. They executed all of the required elements flawlessly and their showmanship earned them standing ovations from the crowd and chants of "6.0." Pelletier was so proud of his performance that he knelt down and kissed the ice when it was over. But when the marks came in, their enthusiasm burst. Five of the nine judges (Russia, China, Ukraine, Poland and France) had placed them second. The Russian skaters were going to win the gold and the Canadians would have to be satisfied with silver.

While the athletes resigned themselves to their second place finish, the media and numerous Olympic officials objected. The Canadian pair was immediately hounded by the press, receiving nearly 200 requests a day for interviews and television appearances. The day after winning their silver medal, Salé and Pelletier conducted 13 straight hours of interviews. Each time they responded diplomatically and with humour, discussing how proud they were of their performance, but avoided comments about the judging. Their modesty and charm won over both the media and the public. Salé and Pelletier became the stars of the Games, gaining more coverage than all other medalists. At the same time, their circumstances placed judging in the sport of figure skating under the microscope.

Ron Pfenning, the American referee, held a meeting with the judges the next day. The French judge, Marie-Reine Le Gougne, blurted out that she had been pressured by Didier Gailhaguet, the head of the French Olympic Committee, to place the Russians first in a deal that would guarantee votes for the French ice dancers, Marina Anissina and Gwendel Peizerat. Le Gougne also had other potential motives for bowing to the pressure — she was one of the candidates being considered for the ISU's technical committee and needed the support of Eastern bloc countries. She later recanted her statement and changed her story numerous times during the investigation. On February 14, the ISU voted unanimously to suspend Le Gougne for misconduct. If Le Gougne's marks were excluded, Salé and Pelletier would be placed in an exact tie with the Russian pair. But the ISU decided that her suspension should have no effect on the marks since a judge's decision is final and cannot be reversed.

The Canadians, particularly Dick Pound, vice-president of the IOC, lobbied the International Olympic Committee's president, Dr. Jacques Rogge. They argued that this incident could have an effect not just on figure skating, but on the larger world of competitive sport. Therefore it needed to be resolved quickly to restore the sport's integrity. The IOC's executive board voted on February 15 and by a vote of seven to one it decided to award a second set of gold medals to the Canadian pair. It was only the fourth time such a decision had been made in Olympic history. Salé and Pelletier were also chosen as the Canadian flag bearers for the closing ceremonies.

Jamie Salé and David Pelletier decided to turn professional shortly after the Olympic Games. Within a few weeks, they signed a multi-year contract to join both the Canadian and American "Stars on Ice" tours. Their charm, humour and mature handling of the scandal and the constant media attention that surrounded their Olympic experience made them heroes both on and off the ice. They were chosen as spokespersons for numerous products, including Roots fashions. Their perfect performance earned them the title of Canadian Pairs Team of the Year at the Canadian Sports Awards.

Salé and Pelletier's Olympic roller coaster ride may lead to a substantial reform of the voting system for future figure skating events. Shortly after the scandal, the International Skating Union proposed an overhaul to the marking and scoring system to eliminate vote swapping and corruption. If the proposal succeeds, Salé and Pelletier will be partly responsible for ensuring that in figure skating, future golden performances will result in gold medals.

ACKNOWLEDGEMENTS

I COULD NOT HAVE completed this book without the help and support of family, friends, colleagues, the athletes themselves and numerous sports associations.

The hardest step with any new project is just convincing yourself to start and then to continue working on it each day. There is no guarantee that your work will be published or that it will attract a large audience. The support and encouragement of many friends and family members helped me to perservere. This book likely would not have become a reality without Bruce McDougall, a professional writer, editor and friend. He prompted me to continue writing, suggested a suitable publisher, Raincoast, and did an initial edit of the first half of the text. I want to thank many close friends for their enthusiasm and support for this project, which further entrenched my conviction that the stories should be shared with a wider audience. My parents, Sharon and John Zeiler; in-laws, Andrea and Harry Bricks; as well as my brother Brian, his fiancée Sarah, and my brothers and sisters-in-law Hartley, Wendy, Steven and Stacey, all rallied around the idea. John, Sharon, Harry and Andrea were particularly helpful in providing babysitting services throughout the process. My father also played a part in providing the title for this book — each athlete profiled herein has shown that it takes heart to achieve the gold standard in his or her sport. My wife Shari provided continued support throughout this endeavour even though on many occasions it led me to neglect certain responsibilities at home, such as our weed-infested garden. She also acted as my first-round editor for every story written. Avery, my adorable daughter, played the important role of stress breaker — her laughter causes anyone to forget their worries and smile.

The athletes themselves were the models for these exciting and inspiring stories. In particular, I want to thank all the athletes who gave their time for interviews, follow-up questions and photos: Doug Anakin, Arnold Boldt, Gaétan Boucher, Sharon Donnelly, Sylvie Fréchette, George

Hungerford, Dr. Roger Jackson, Silken Laumann, Lawrence Lemieux, Alwyn Morris, Anne Ottenbrite, Chrissy Redden and Beckie Scott. Historians and fans also aided me a great deal in my research: Ron Hotchkiss, Ann White and Brian Luftspring, and from the Canadian Broadcasting Corporation, Michael Drapek, Paul Harrington and Paula Nielson. Many journalists, authors and internet content providers unknowingly contributed to the project by supplying me with the background information to craft these 21 profiles. Thank you as well to the many Canadian athletic societies that helped in providing background material, contact information, or photographs, particularly: Rowing Canada, Speed Skating Canada, Triathlon Canada, Cycling Canada, Canadian Paralympics Association, Skate Canada, the Canadian Olympic Association and the Canadian Sports Hall of Fame. Allan, Jackson and Debbie from the Canadian Sports Hall of Fame, thank you for the use of your files for research and loaning many of the photos in the hall's extensive collection for this project.

Special thanks to my lawyer and friend Jordan Jacobs for all of his help in negotiating my contract, marketing suggestions and general support. Lastly, the staff at Raincoast Books has been instrumental in designing, editing, marketing and polishing *Hearts of Gold*. In particular, I would like to thank Jesse Finkelstein, Rights and Contracts Manager; Michelle Benjamin, Publisher; Tom Best, National Accounts Manager; Teresa Bubela, Designer; and especially Simone Doust, my editor. Without her help, drive, enthusiasm and many suggestions and edits, these stories would not be as entertaining and my vision would not have been captured as clearly.

PHOTO CREDITS

BIBLIOGRAPHY AND SOURCES

BOOKS

Batten, Jack. *1896-1996 Canada at the Olympics: The First 100 Years.* Toronto: INFACT Publishing, 1996.

Connors, Martin, Dupuis, Diane, Morgan, Brad. *The Olympics Factbook: A Spectator's Guide to the Winter and Summer Games.* Detroit: Visible Ink Press, 1992

Dheensaw, Cleve. *Olympics 100: Canada at the Summer Games.* Victoria: Orca Book Publishers, 1996.

Duncanson, Neil. *The Fastest Men On Earth: The 100 metre Olympic Champions.* London: Willow Books, 1988.

Fisher, Douglas & Wise, Syd. *Canada's Sporting Heroes.* Toronto: General Publishing 1977.

Fréchette, Sylvie and Lacroix, Lilianne, translated by Kathe Roth. *Gold at Last.* Toronto: Stoddart Publishing, 1983.

Luftspring, Sammy. *Call Me Sammy,* Scarborough, Ontario: Prentice-Hall of Canada Ltd., 1975.

Medrick, Robin and Thomas, Wendy (editors). *Heroes in Our Midst: Top Canadian Athletes Share Personal Stories From Their Lives in Sports.* Toronto: McClelland & Stewart Ltd., 2001.

Morrow, Don, Keyes, Merry, Simpson, Wayne, Cosentino, Frank and Lappage, Ron. *A Concise History of Sports in Canada.* Toronto: Oxford University Press, 1989.

Ondaatje, Christopher and Currie, Gordon. *Olympic Victory: the story behind the Canadian bobsled club's incredible victory at the 1964 Winter Olympic Games.* Toronto, Pagurian Press Limited, 1967.

Page, James. *Black Olympian Medalists.* Englewood, California: Libraries Unlimited Inc., 1991.

Roxborough, Henry. *Canada at the Olympic Games.* Toronto: McGraw-Hill Ryerson Limited, 1975.

Smith, Beverly. *Gold on Ice: The Salé and Pelletier Story*. Toronto: Key Porter Books, 2002.

Stojko, Elvis and Châtaigneau, Gérard. *Heart and Soul*. Toronto: Rocketeer Publishing Inc., 1997.

Strudwick, Leslie. *Athletes*. New York: Crabtree Publishing, 1999.

Wallechinsky, David. *The Complete Book of the Summer Olympics*. New York: The Overlook Press, 2000.

NEWSPAPERS AND MAGAZINES

The Beaver	*Saturday Night Magazine*
Canadian Jewish News	*Ski Trax Magazine*
Canoeing	*Sporting Life*
Capher Journal	*Sports Illustrated*
Edmonton Sun	*Toronto Star*
Globe and Mail	*Toronto Sun*
Montreal Gazette	*Weekend Magazine*

ASSOCIATIONS

Aboriginal Sport Circle
    www.aboriginalsportscircle.ca
BC Sports Hall of Fame
    www.bcsportshalloffame.com
Canadian Association for the Advancement of Women and Sport
and Physical Activity
    www.caaws.ca
Canadian Cycling Association
    www.canadian-cycling.com
Canadian Canoe Association
    www.canoekayak.ca/
Canadian Olympic Association
    www.coa.ca
Canadian Paralympic Committee
    www.paralympic.ca
Canadian Yachting Association
    www.sailing.ca

Rowing Canada
    www.rowingcanada.org
Skate Canada
    www.skatecanada.ca
Speed Skating Canada
    www.speedskating.ca
Swim Ontario
    www.swimontario.com
Triathlon Canada
    www.triathloncanada.com
Canada's Sports Hall of Fame

INTERNET

Amputee Online
    www.amputee-online.com
Canoe
    www. slam.canoe.ca/
CBC Millenium Series, The Olympians
    www.cbc.ca/sports/olympians
Jaime Sale and David Pelletier
    www.sale-pelletier.com
Mountain Bike Racer
    www.mountainbikeracer.com
National Library of Canada
    www.nlc-bnc.ca
Sharon Donnelly
    www.sharondonnelly.com
Silken Laumann
    www.silkenlaumann.com

INDEX

ABOUT THE AUTHOR

LORNE ZEILER is active in the financial industry and business community, and is also a prolific writer. His articles have appeared in both Canadian and international financial journals including the *Globe and Mail Report on Business*, *Canadian Treasurer* and *CFA Digest*. He is also a regular lecturer at York University. Lorne lives in Toronto with his wife, Shari, and his daughter, Avery.